André Kertész

André Kertész

Introduction by Danièle Sallenave

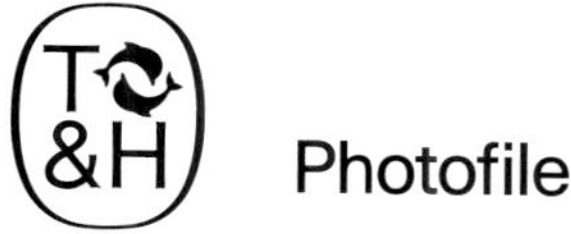

The Photofile series is the original
English-language edition of the
Photo Poche collection. It was
first published between 1986 and
1992 by the Centre National de
la Photographie, Paris, with the
support of the French Ministry of
Culture. Robert Delpire (1926–2017)
was the creator of the series and
its managing editor until 2017.

Cover design and typesetting by Matthew Young

Translated from the French by Sheila Chevallier
and Marianne Tinnell-Faure

First published in the United Kingdom in 2007 by
Thames & Hudson Ltd, 181A High Holborn, London
WC1V 7QX

First published in the United States of America in
2007 by Thames & Hudson Inc., 500 Fifth Avenue,
New York, New York 10110

Reprinted 2017, 2021

Photo Poche © 2007 Actes Sud, France
Photographs © Ministère de la Culture,
Association française pour la diffusion
du patrimoine photographique, Paris
English translation © 1986 Centre National
de la Photographie
This edition © 2007 Thames & Hudson Ltd, London

British Library Cataloguing-in-Publication Data
A catalogue record for this book is available from
the British Library

Library of Congress Control Number 2007900793

ISBN: 978-0-500-41063-9
Printed and bound in Italy

To see is to read

An idea in vogue has it that the artist must necessarily be in opposition to his language, that he has to force it, constrain it, and twist its syntax in order to mould it to his own design. However, another definition of art is perhaps not only possible but more accurate – that the real artist is someone who has been able, through patient work or with immediate insight, to discover the profound nature of the language he has chosen and its laws, and to fully exploit its forms of expression, from the most obvious to the most hidden.

These two types of artist will always be in opposition. The first lives in a state of continual conflict between his ego and his language, while the second is constantly learning about the increasing concordance of his language and his world. For, if he carries it to its limits, the analysis of his art's essential forms necessarily leads him to discover the bonds of secret suitability linking it to certain objects of the world, and, moreover, that the laws of his art are perhaps those of the world itself, and that art is their revelator.

This is no doubt the motivating intuition that inspires the meaning and is the driving force behind the work of André Kertész. From the beginning, the artist seems to have discovered and established that, by its very nature, black and white photography was destined to become much more than a simple mode of figurative representation and that the way it represents things makes it a mode of understanding the world. This is not only because photography, like painting, cuts up the world, frames and immobilizes it, reducing it to two of its three natural dimensions, but also because black and white photography substitutes for colours an abstract scale of gradations from absolute black to brilliant white. Black and white photography thus immediately lends itself to a reading of the world such as Arago gave it. It doesn't merely register it or record its reflection, but brings it back to its essential aspects of shapes, features, contrasts, shadows and shading. Torn away from the arbitrariness of movement (which, according to Baudelaire, 'displaces the lines') and the changing shimmer of colour, the world photographed in black and white undergoes an abstraction which makes it more understandable. There is a nascent organization of people, objects and scenes: the transposition of a fragment of the world and its reproduction in black and white x-rays the world and reveals the embryo of meaning, its sense in the process of forming.

Black and white photography is thus the perfect tool for a concrete analysis and an active intelligibility of the world, especially if the artist has lighter, less clumsy, cameras with precise and rapid lenses. André Kertész's youth and early career in fact coincided with black and white photography becoming portable. One could finally go out into the world to observe it and reveal its laws. Kertész's first photos demonstrated this new realism which led him, inexhaustibly, towards things in a movement of active seizing and understanding. Small farms on the Hungarian plains, the poverty of muddy farmyards, flocks of geese on a road, blind musicians on street corners, shawled women in the shade, runaway horses, rain-shiny pavements: these humble traces, as if they had deposited themselves on the banks of time seem, helped by our nostalgia, to reveal their secret and threatened essence. The strictness of the framing and the infinite melancholy of the greys confer on them the 'surface polish' that Flaubert sought from the use of the imperfect in his sentences. And, though invisible and omnipresent, the photographer shows himself through his art as having been there and having disappeared behind things.

This 'new realism' (which became known as 'new objectivity' after WWI) was like a return to the golden age of photography, a renewal of its baptismal vows. The world can be taken 'as it is', in the science of its contours, in the precision of its lines, in bright contrast and clear-cut shadows. The photographer is someone who goes towards the world, not to trouble it with his subjectivity, but to respond to the demand for expression he is able to read in it. The world wants to be fixed on the plate to ensure its survival, its existence perhaps, but above all its intelligibility, even if it is sometimes necessary to contribute to it by having, for example, a man silhouetted on a lighted wall so his solitary shadow brings out the meaning of a nighttime alley. The time had come for a return to real things: no more studied fog, gum bichromate, and the claim to be the same as painting. No more quarrels about technique; you have to be there and be the eye. To have the Leica in hand and to seize the moment. Black and white photography is outside, *sur le motif*, and for a long time. The 'motif' is big-city life, sad suburbs, old rooftops in Touraine, bistros and posters.

However, what André Kertész discovered quickly and revealed admirably is the fact that black and white photography nurtures a bond of deep complicity with everything in the natural and artificial world, both literal and figurative, that can be written: posters, advertising, but also wheels, fences, posts in the snow, tracks on the road, shadows in the setting sun, and the lacy outline of foliage on white walls. Black and white photography became the revelator of the world's graphic truth and gave birth to the movement of concrete abstraction, realism and truth which it had borne. It said that the visible is readable, that the world is made of signs to decipher, which are not always words, but ideograms, pictograms, photographs. To see is to read: if black and white photography doesn't have the same sense today, it is not only because of the appearance and development of colour. It is because the links of the visible and readable are attached in a totally different way; we are no longer as sure that meaning is what can be read and that reading is the great game through which the world can be deciphered.

To see is to read: the symbolic image would perhaps be that of little Ernest, standing in front of the blackboard in his schoolboy's smock, his hand resting near the chalk-smeared slate; or that of a woman's profile on the wall and the painted profiles of the posters; or, closer to us and more abstractly, the stream of black umbrellas seemingly directed by the white arrow painted on the street, seen from the window of a room above. Exactly, *seen from a window*: because while André Kertész shares stylistic characteristics with other photographers (of whom he is the master in age), he has one in particular which recurs often enough to become what Leo Spitzer called the 'spiritual etymon' of an artist. This feature is the high-angle shot. There is an impressive number of them in his work. They give Kertész's pictures their peculiar colour, their lively clarity, something like the mark of the alacrity that drives him. The high-angle view lowers the vanishing point, pulls up the backgrounds, placing them at the top of the image: it is the opposite of the illusion of natural perspective in which the planes are gradated and staggered to a fictive background (which painting, since Leonardo da Vinci, has swathed in a blue-tinged mist). The 'window' or overhead perspective – e.g. the Pont des Arts bridge seen from the clock of the Institut de France, the esplanade seen from the first floor of the Eiffel Tower – is like the view at the theatre from the balcony – movements, intentions, locations, and staging are best perceived from there. Everything becomes visible, nothing is forgotten: the world becomes a big page covered by the signs of social writing. Long shadows in the late afternoon sun of a beautiful day, footprints in the snow, light suits alternating with dresses and dark hats, and metal structures sharply outlined: black and white establishes its reign over a world seen from above; it completes the graphic homogenization and the intellectual grasp of the world. The world is a page, but a living one. The view from above is an urban view with, naturally, a little sky and a lot of ground and pavement, where people are passing by, their upright silhouettes often the only verticals in the picture and their shadows sharp obliques. More so than in the street or the bistros, the social comedy is there to read. The high-angle view uncovers the world's mechanics, and like Descartes who, from his window, saw hats that walked, the photographer takes a philosophical, sceptical step back. These fragments of the city, readable in the cold winter sun or in a nighttime light, seemed as necessary and absurd to him as the path followed by a line of marching ants.

Unlike the medieval artist who tried to adopt 'God's eye' by using multiple contradictory perspectives and by ignoring the relative scale of objects, the Renaissance artist puts the world at 'man's height' by proposing to build it according to the rules of geometric perspective with a horizon and a single vanishing point. But high-angle views were often necessary if he wanted to avoid a jumble of planes and arrange them legibly. The artist-photographer implements this successfully when he combines the high-angle shot with the reduction of the world's images to their graphic size. It helps to make the photographer a witness more than an actor; it abstracts him from the world in movement and enables him to decode it. At his window, he is present in the world without being involved in it; he doesn't walk on the same ground as those he will soon join. He keeps his distance from them in order to look at and understand them. He reads the world more than he sees it; the distance he establishes between things and himself is the condition for their intelligibility. This position, backed up by a philosophical stance, undoubtedly suited André Kertész's personality and temperament, for he chose to live in a studio with a panoramic view of New York. But when, with precise attention, he angled down on others, to capture a twin reflection in the eyes of a child and those of a young dog, or to photograph Mondrian's or Chagall's table, on which objects were placed as in their paintings, the same movement was already present, that of an articulate absence, or an aloof presence. Looking at his work, one could say that the photographer persuaded himself very early on that things offer themselves only to the one who knows how to keep his distance. Everything then becomes clear, easy, decipherable. And the world finally consents to admit that, in reality, it is just *a big book*.

Danièle Sallenave

1. Budapest, 1915.

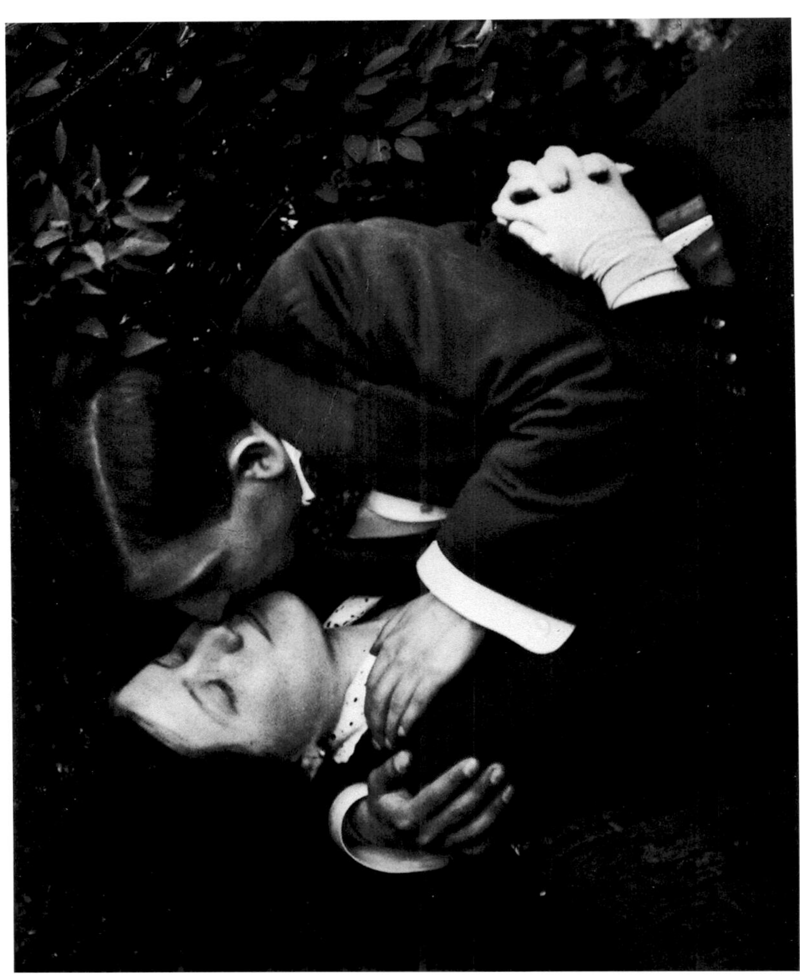

2. Budapest, 1914.

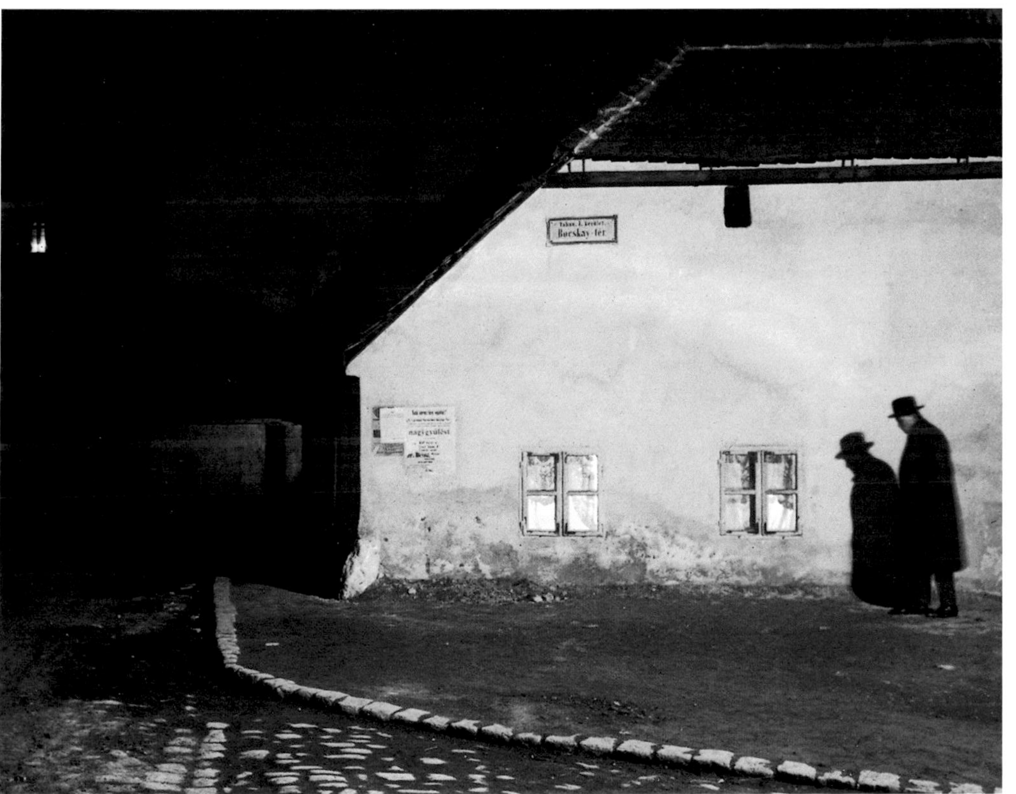
Tabán, I. kerület
Bocskay-tér
nagygyűlést

3. Accordionist, Esztergom, Hungary, 1916.

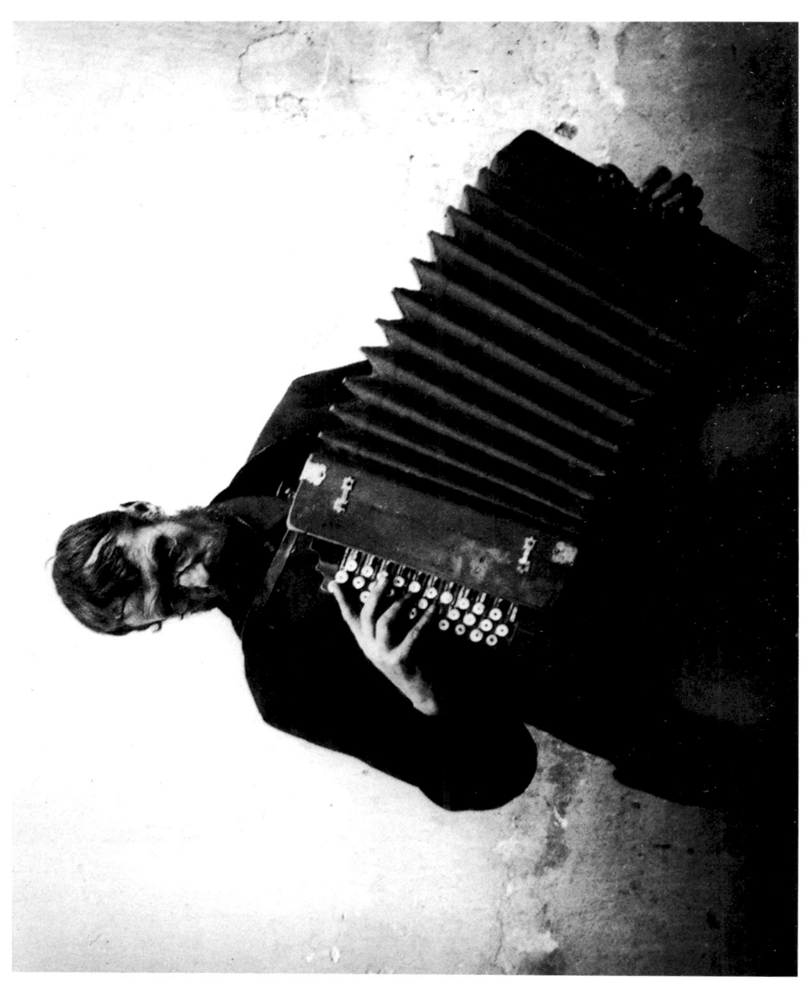

4. Blind musician, Abony, Hungary, 1921.

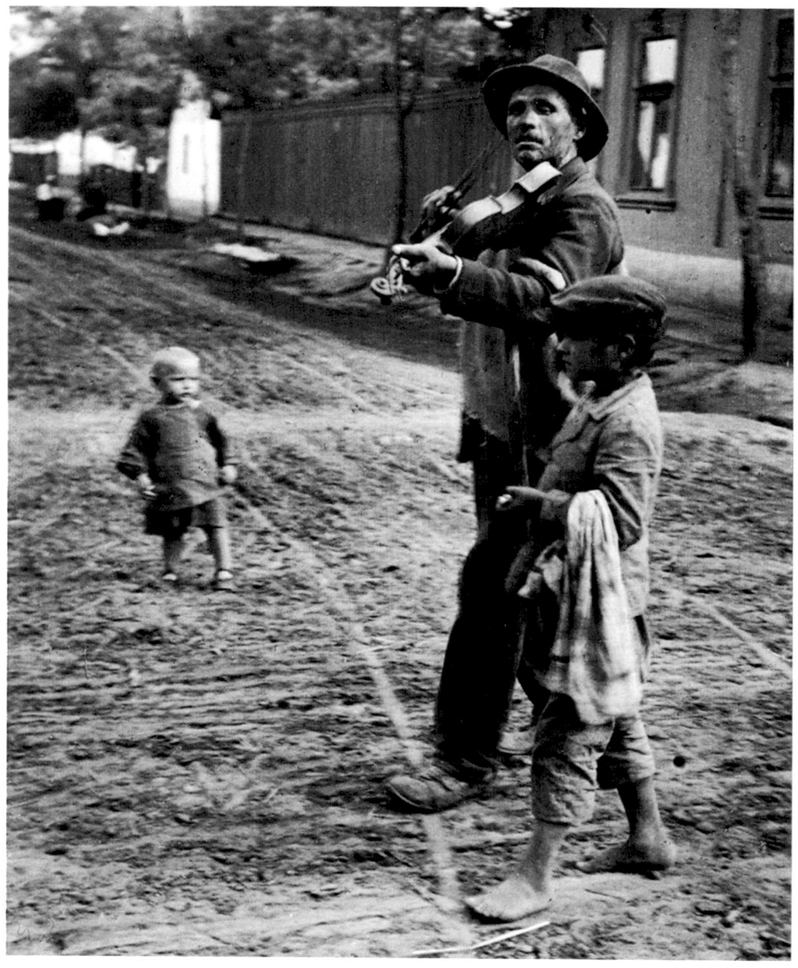

5. Cock fight, Hungary, 1920.

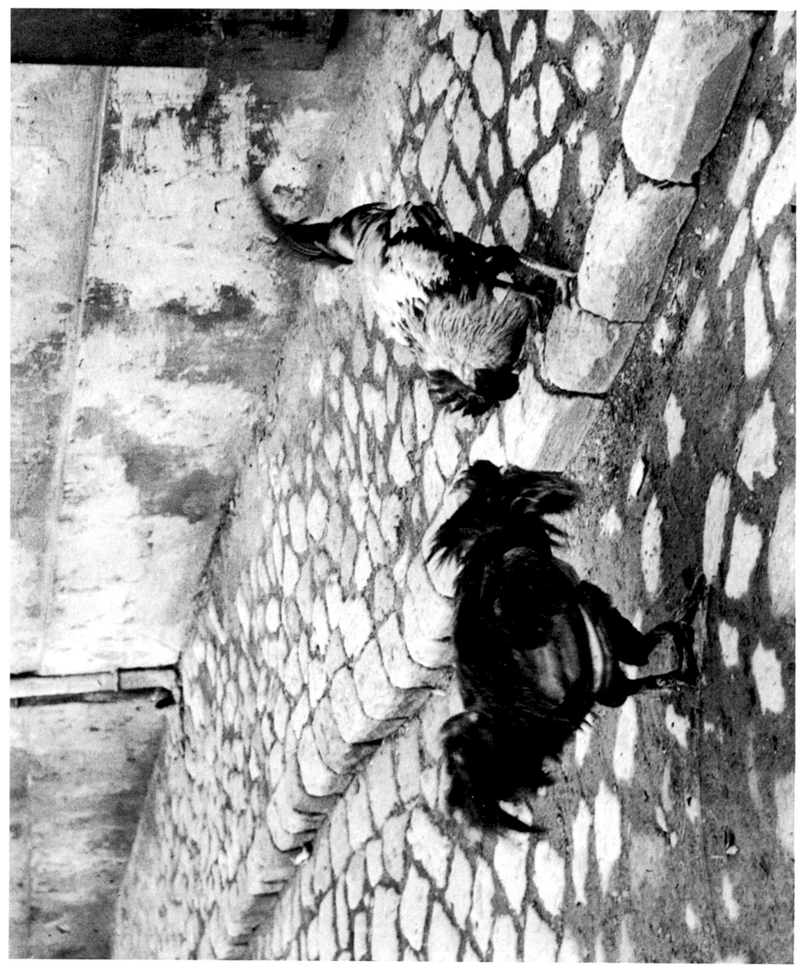

6. Budafok, Hungary, 1919.

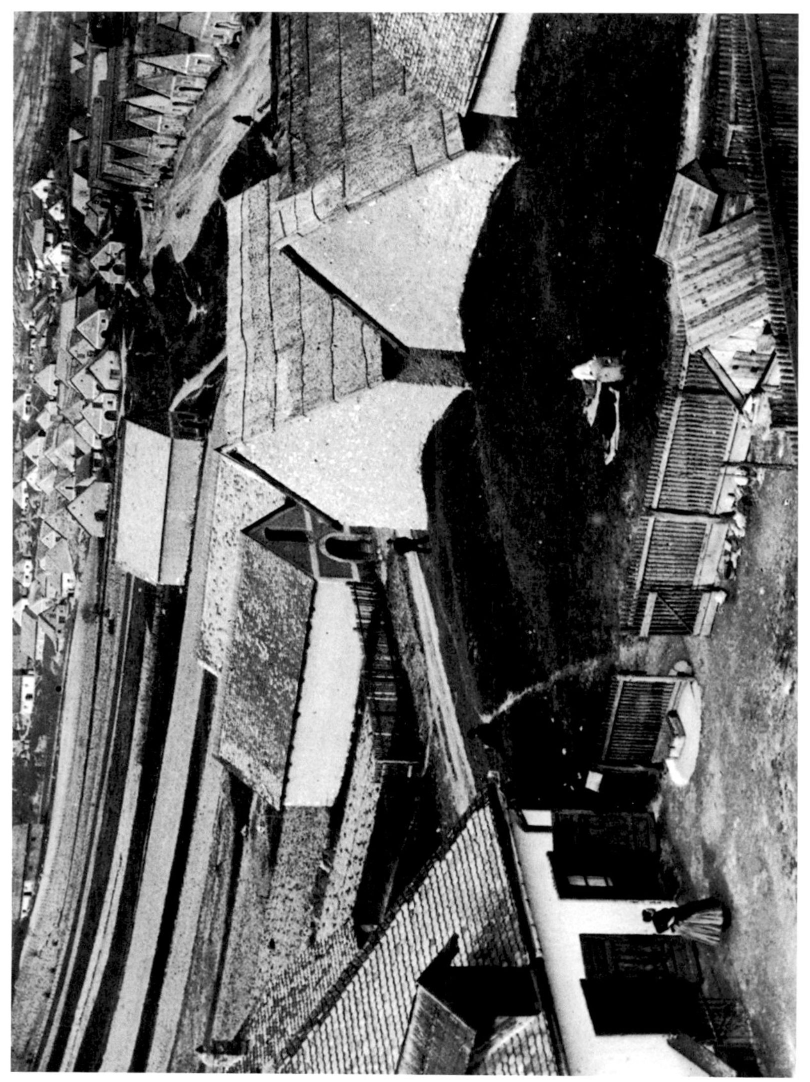

7. Tisza-Szalka, Hungary, 1924.

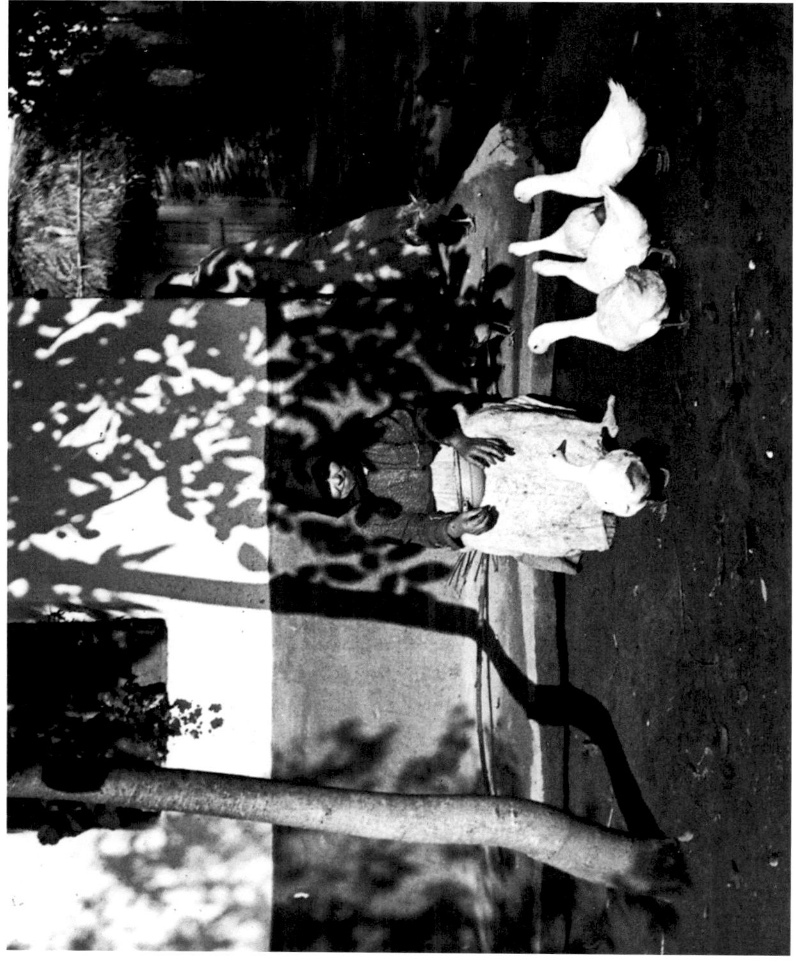

8. Duna Haraszti, Hungary, 1920.

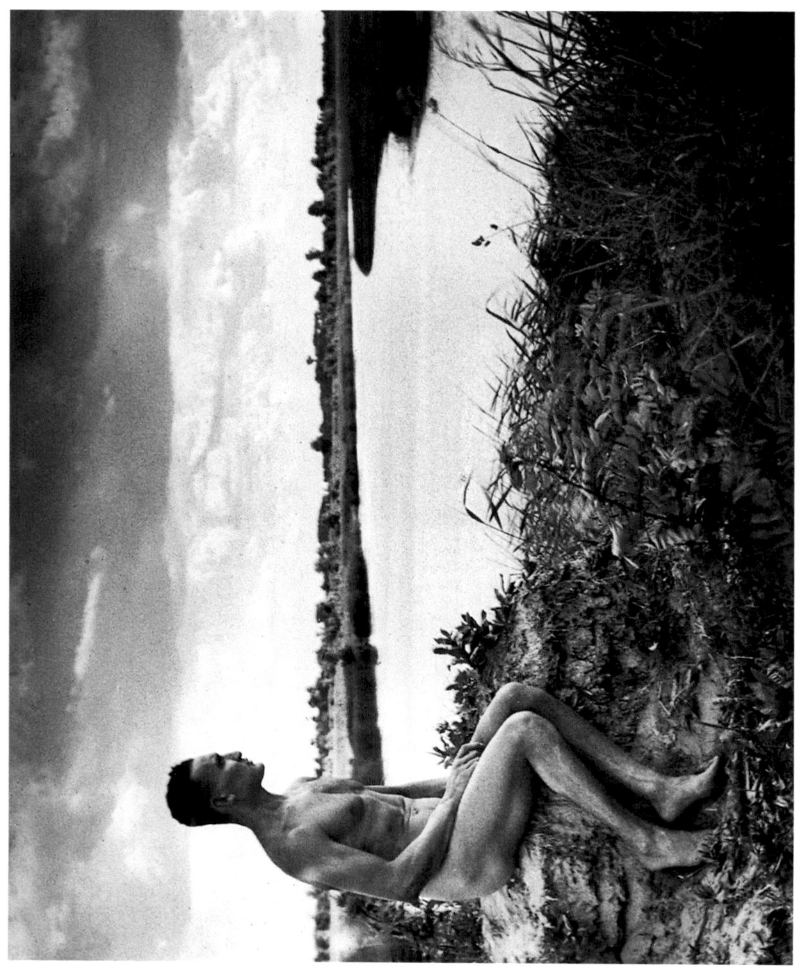

9. Savoie, France, 1929.

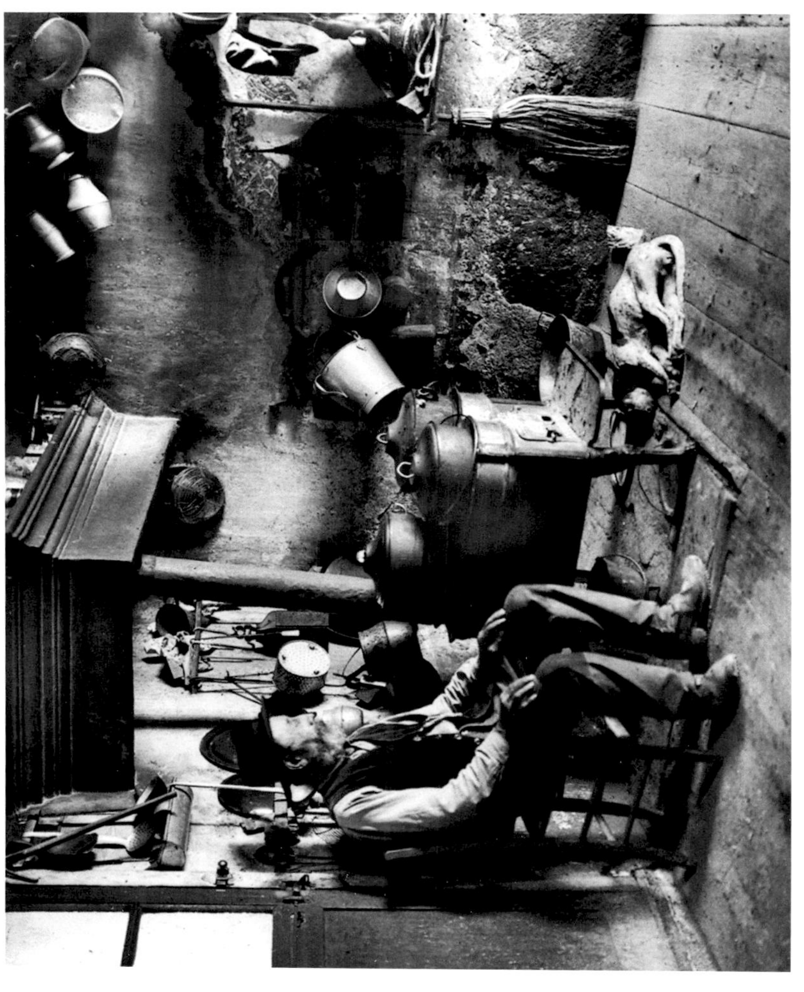

10. Savoie, France, 1929.

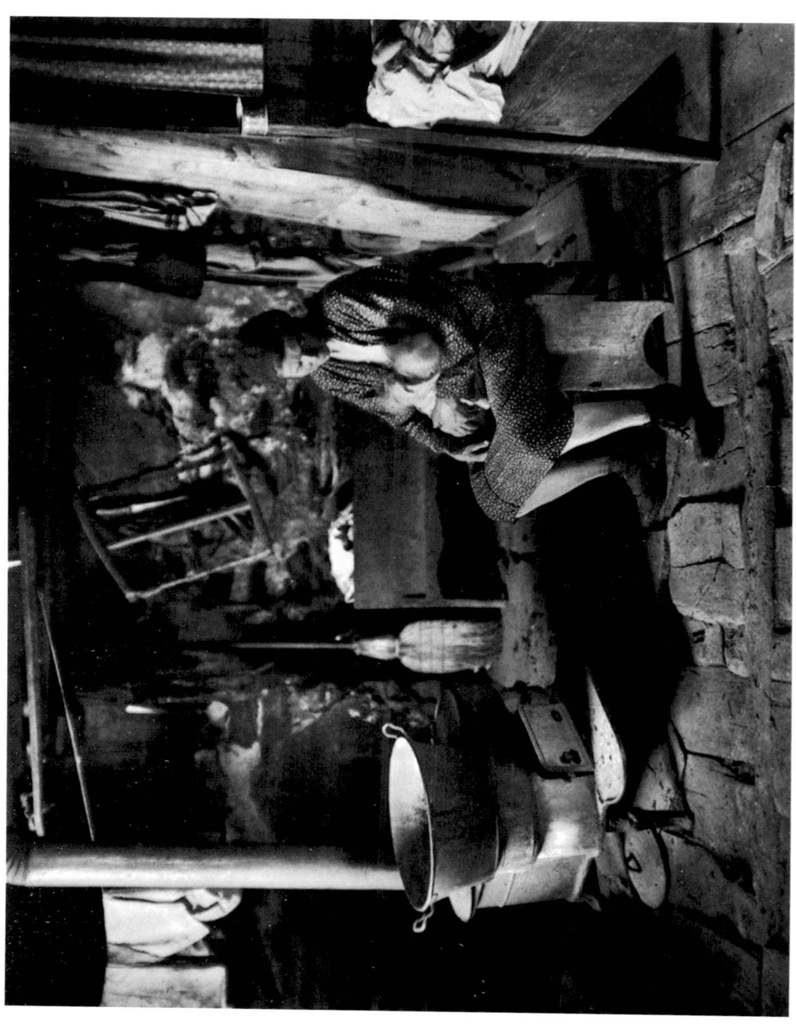

11. Circus, Budapest, 1920.

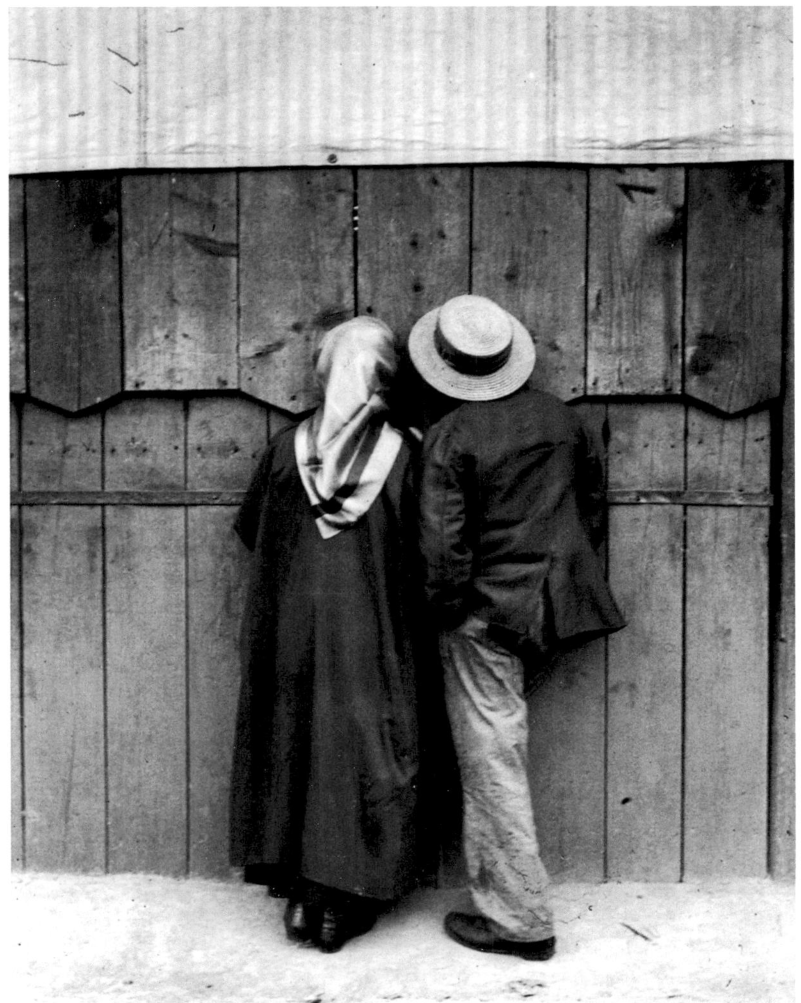

12. Paris, 1925.

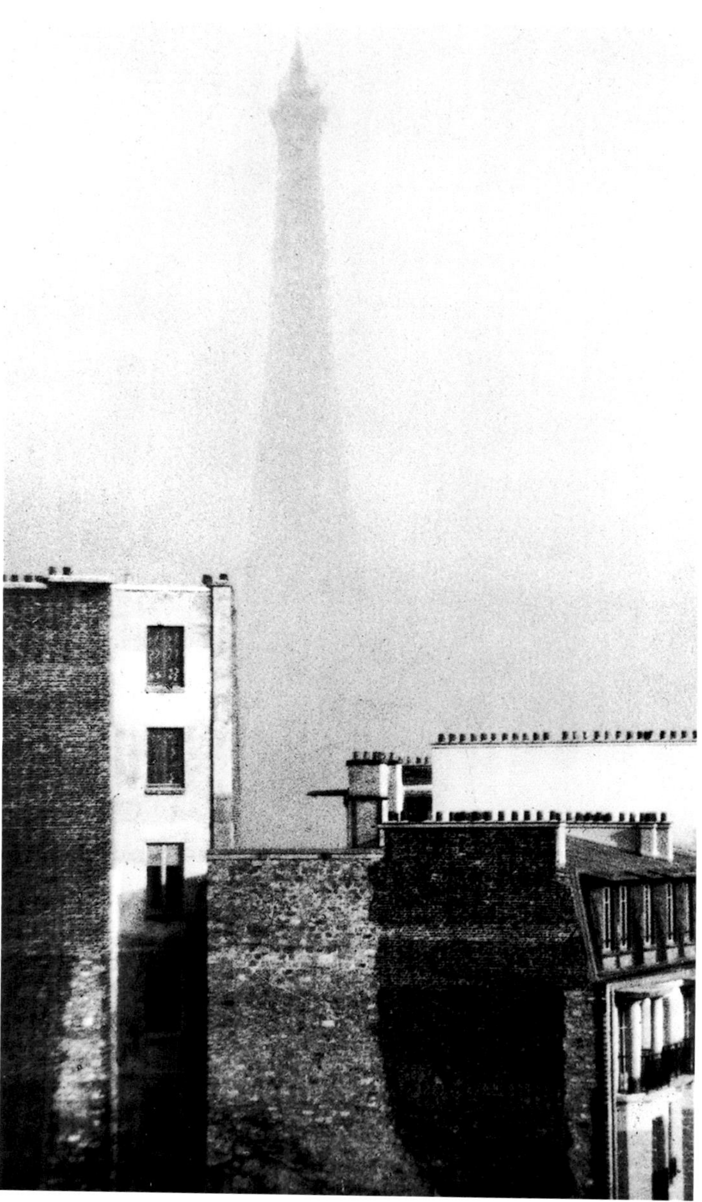

13. Le Café du Dôme, Paris, 1925.

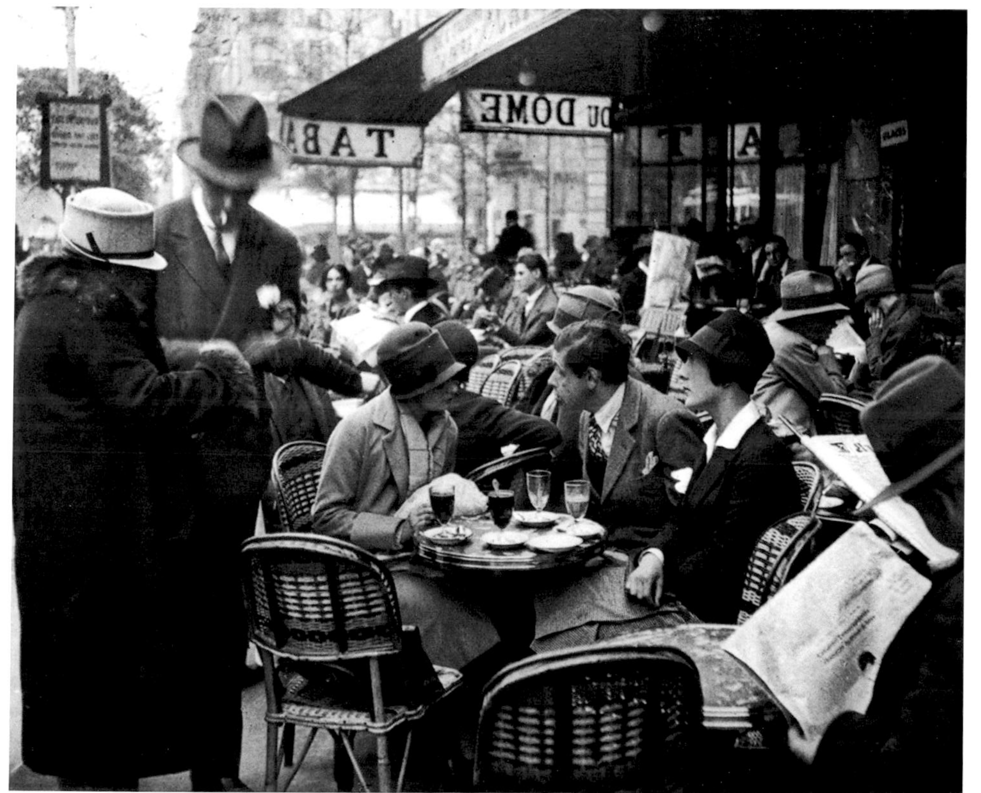
DU DOME
TABAC

14. Paris, 1925.

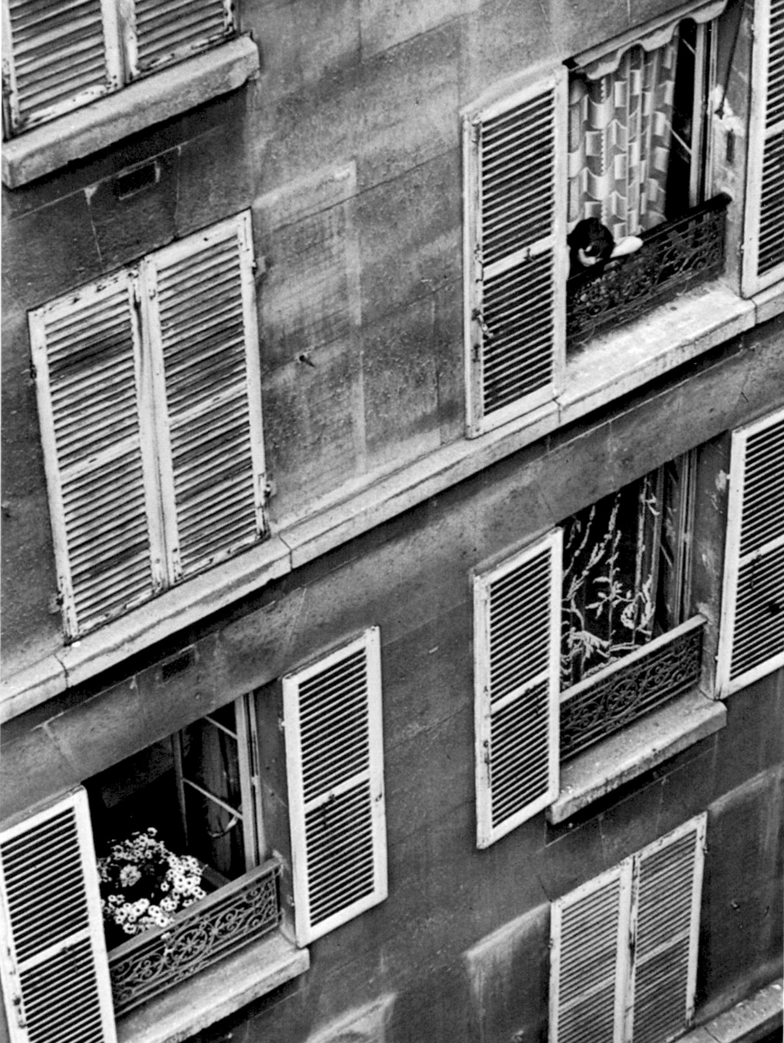

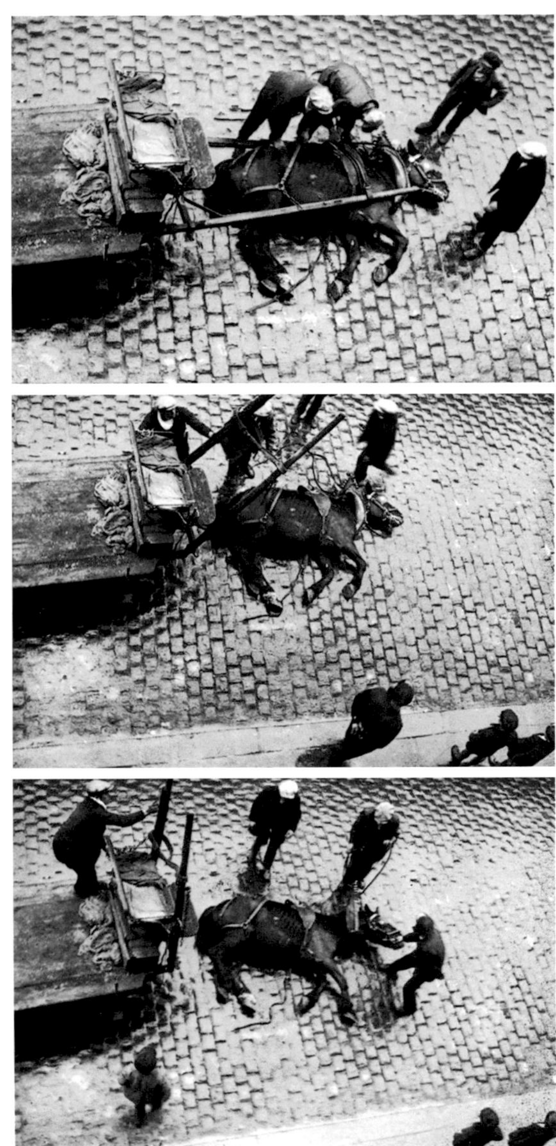

15. Horse sequence, Paris, 1927.

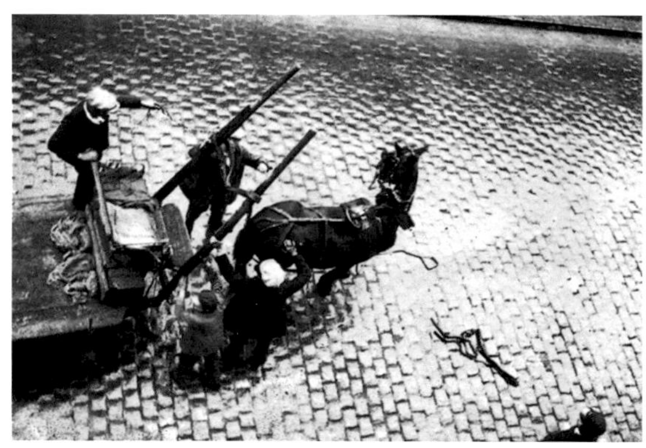

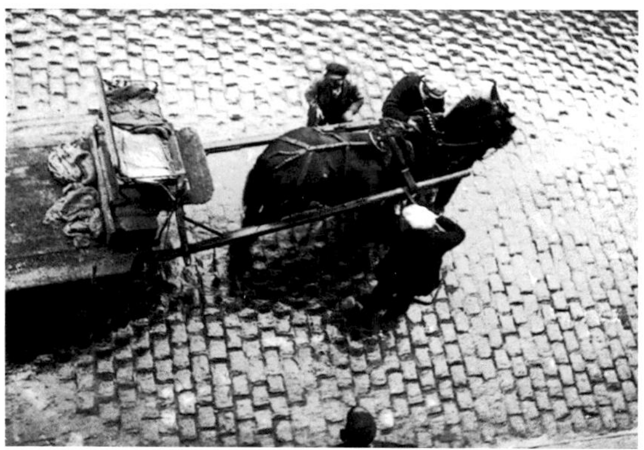

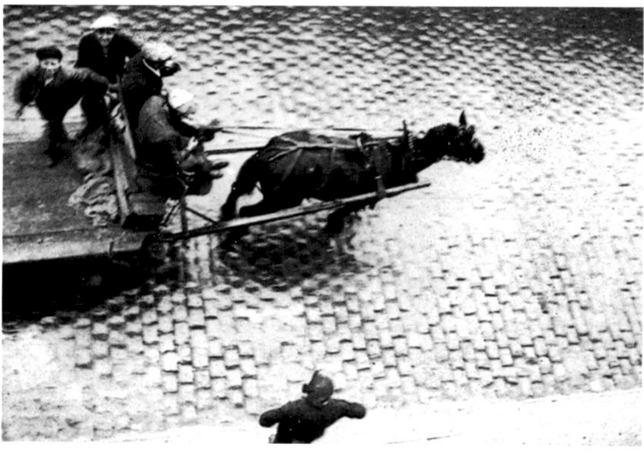

16. Street fair, Paris, 1927.

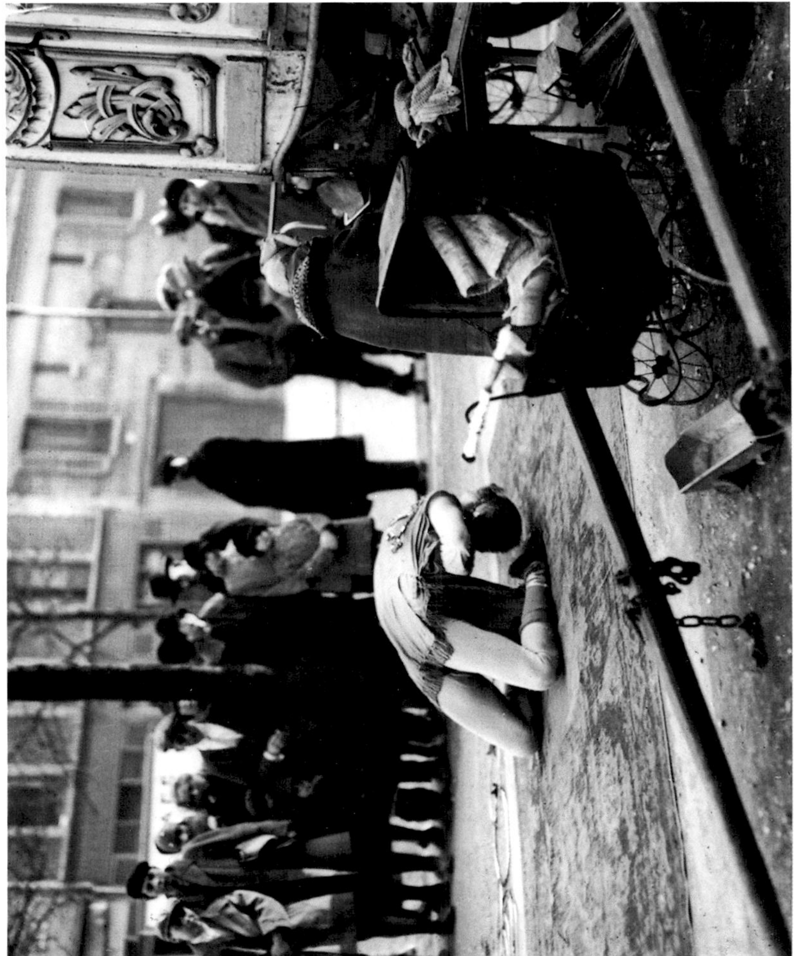

17. Animal market, Saint-Michel, Paris, 1927.

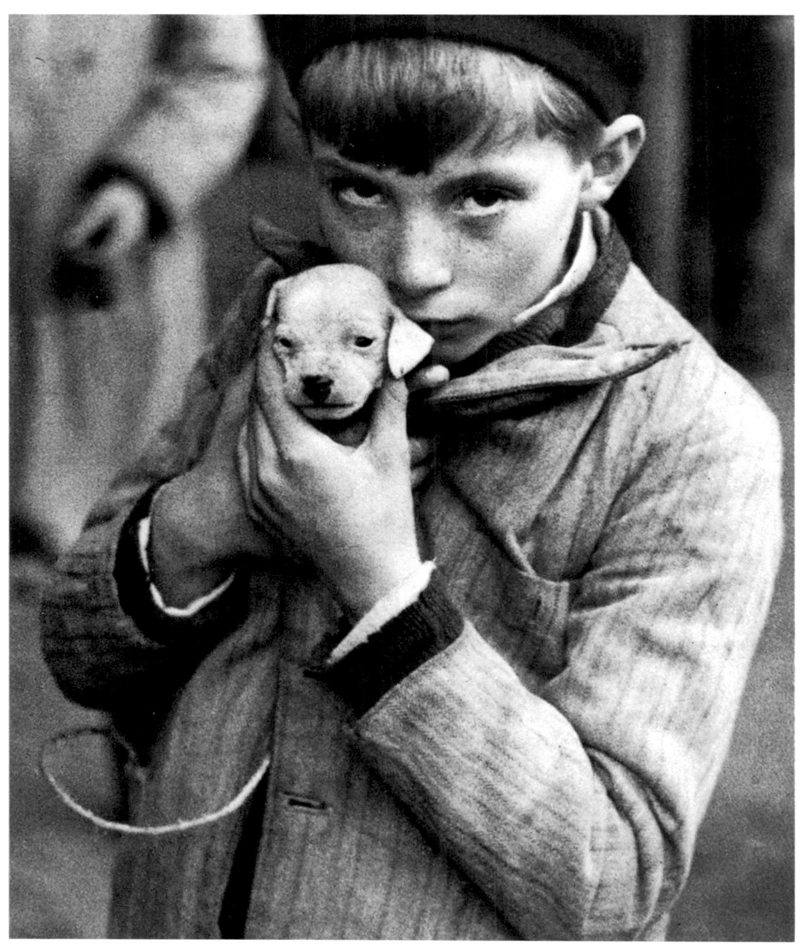

18. The Fork, Paris, 1928.

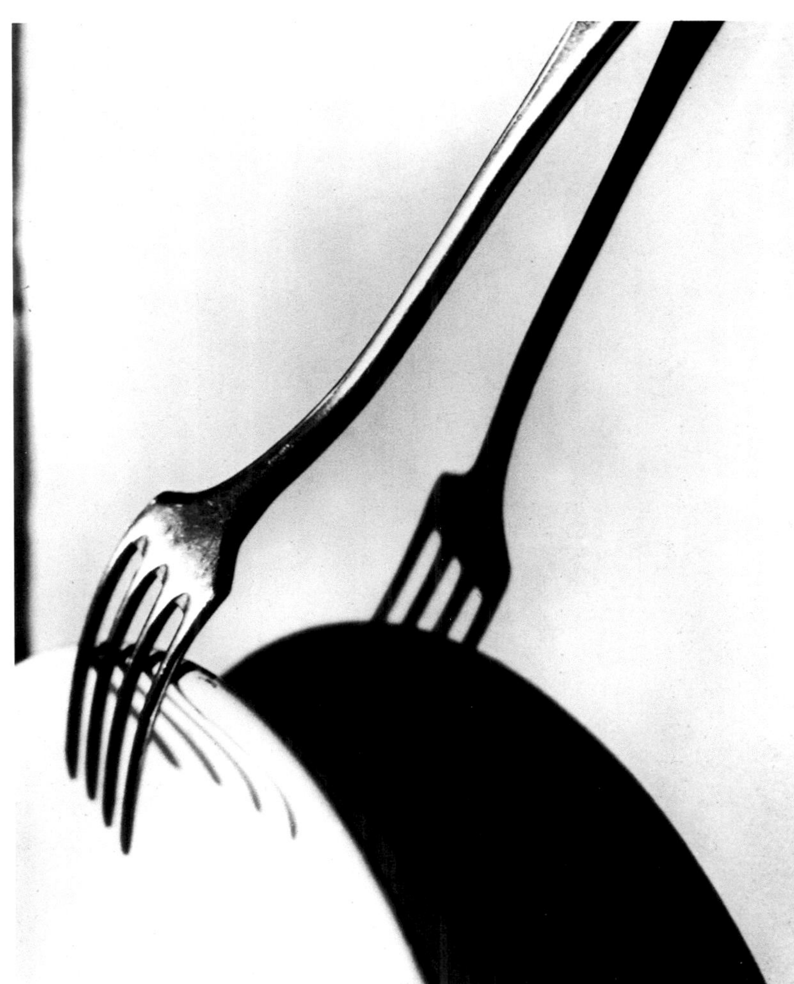

19. At the home of Ilka and Eva Révai, Paris, 1927.

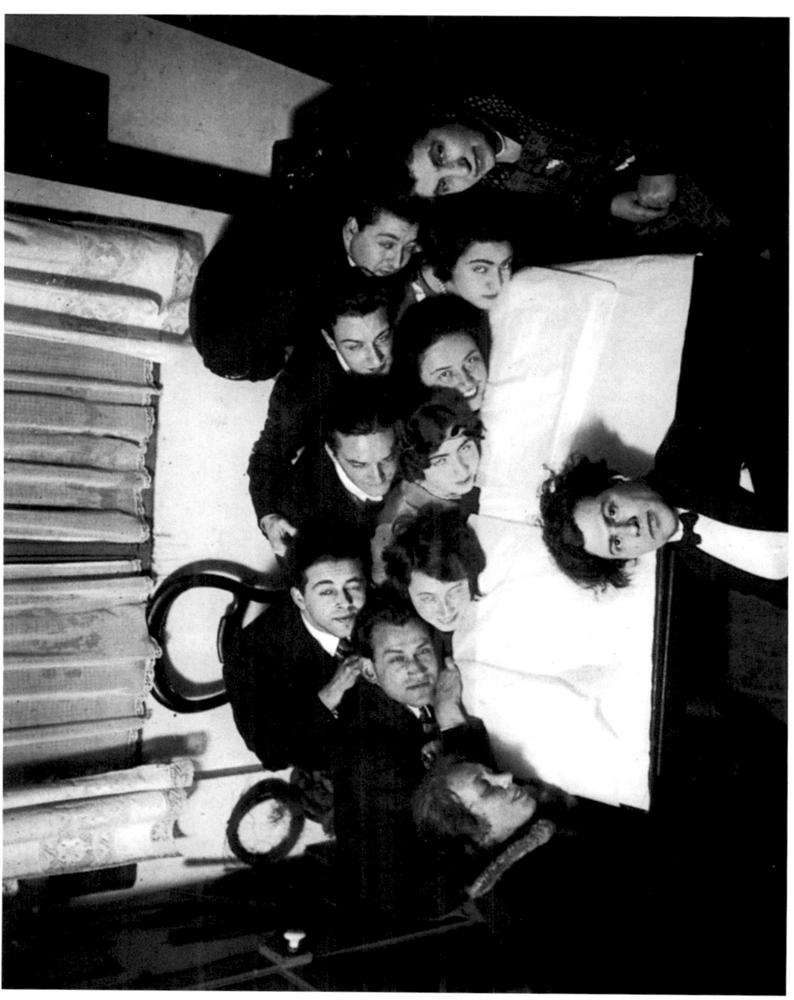

20. Mondrian's studio, Paris, 1926.

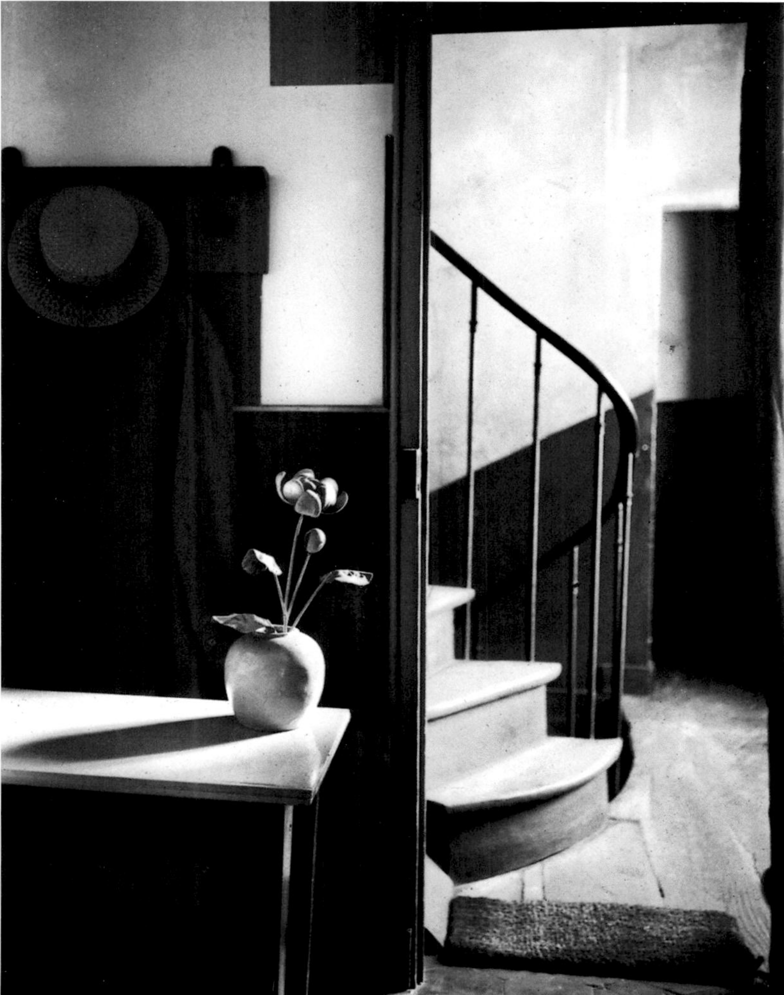

21. Burlesque dancer, Paris, 1926.

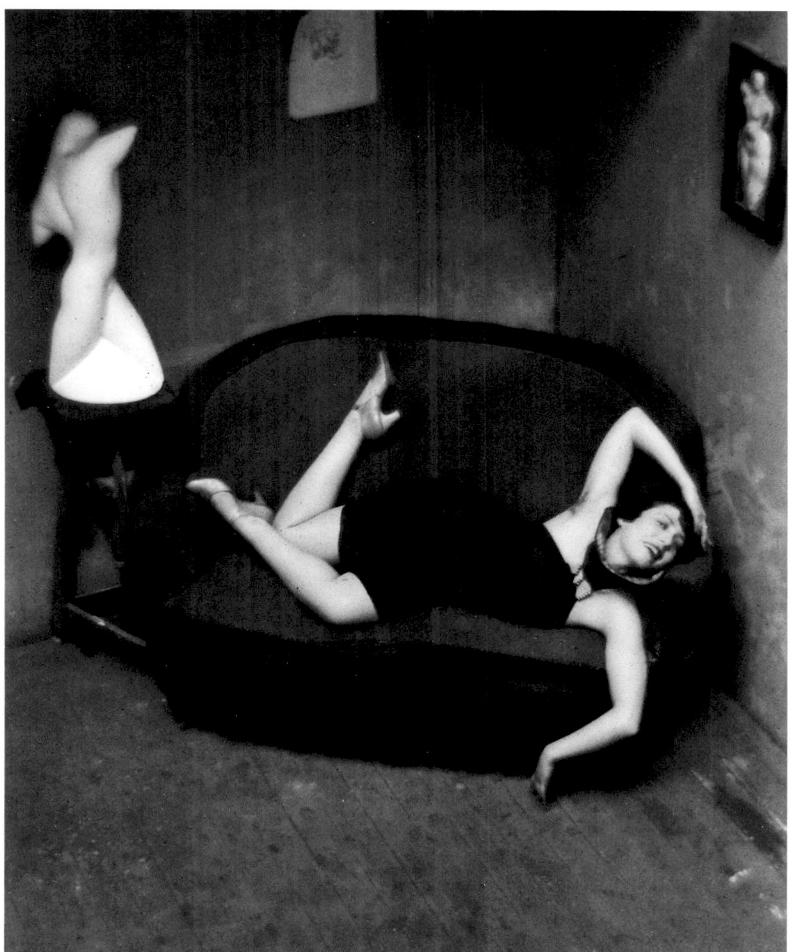

22. Distortion no. 6, 1933.

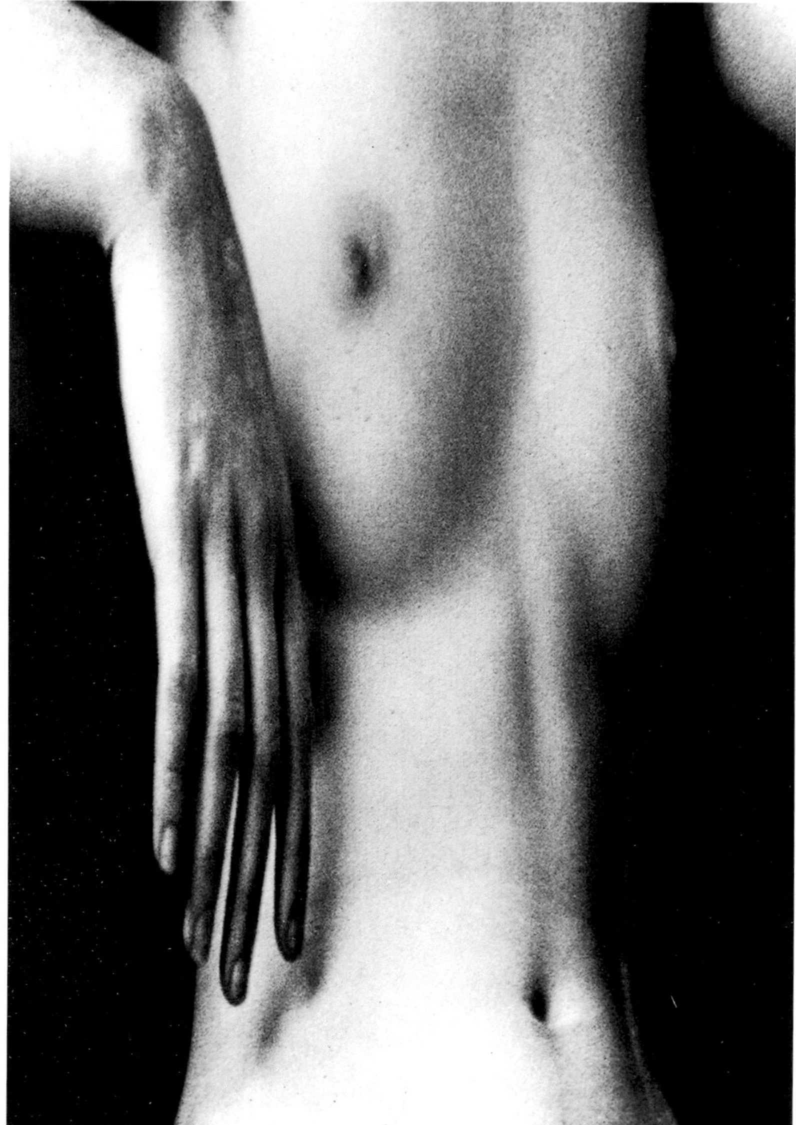

23. Distortion no. 40, 1933.

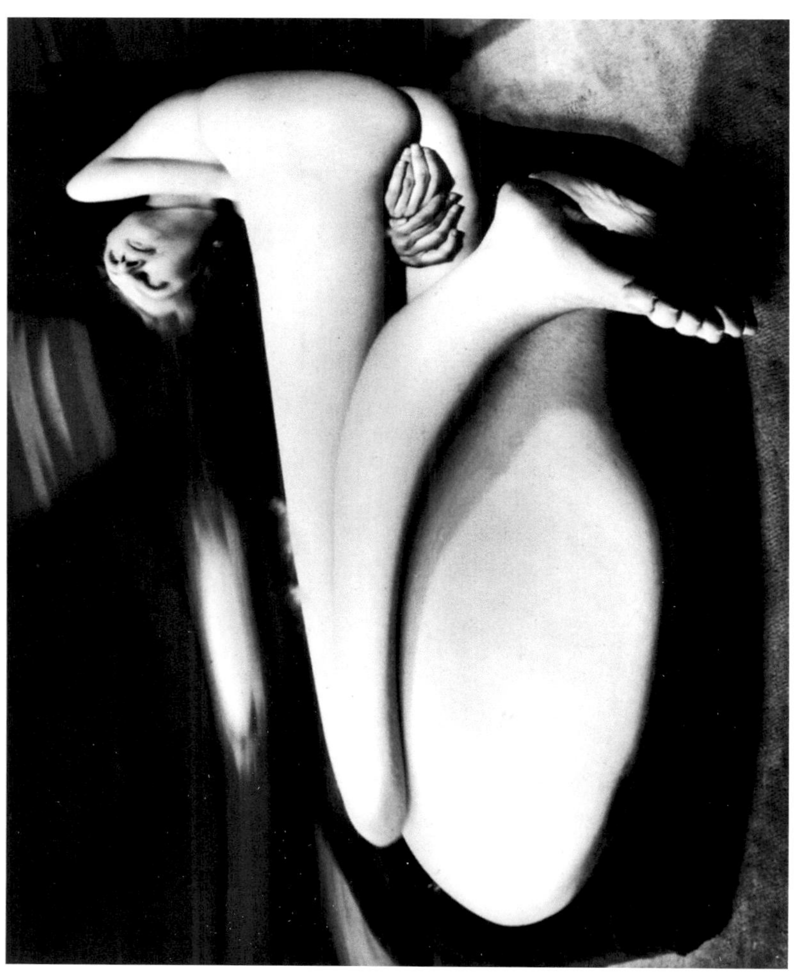

24. Chagall with his family, Paris, 1933.

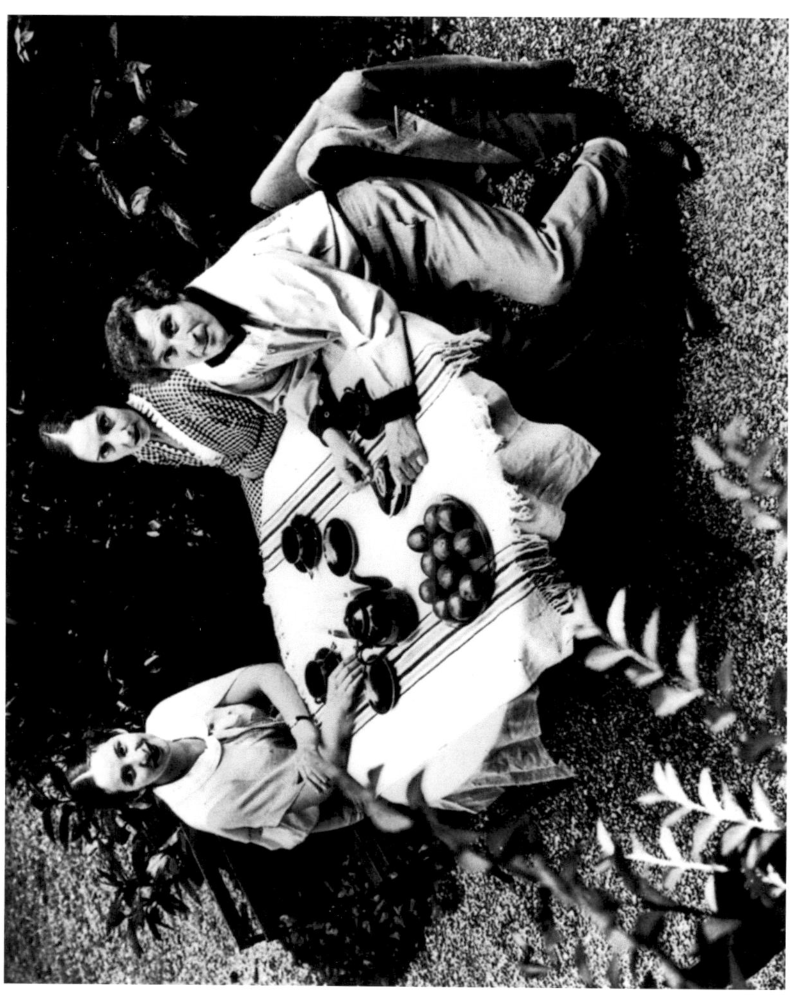

25. Eisenstein, Paris, 1929.

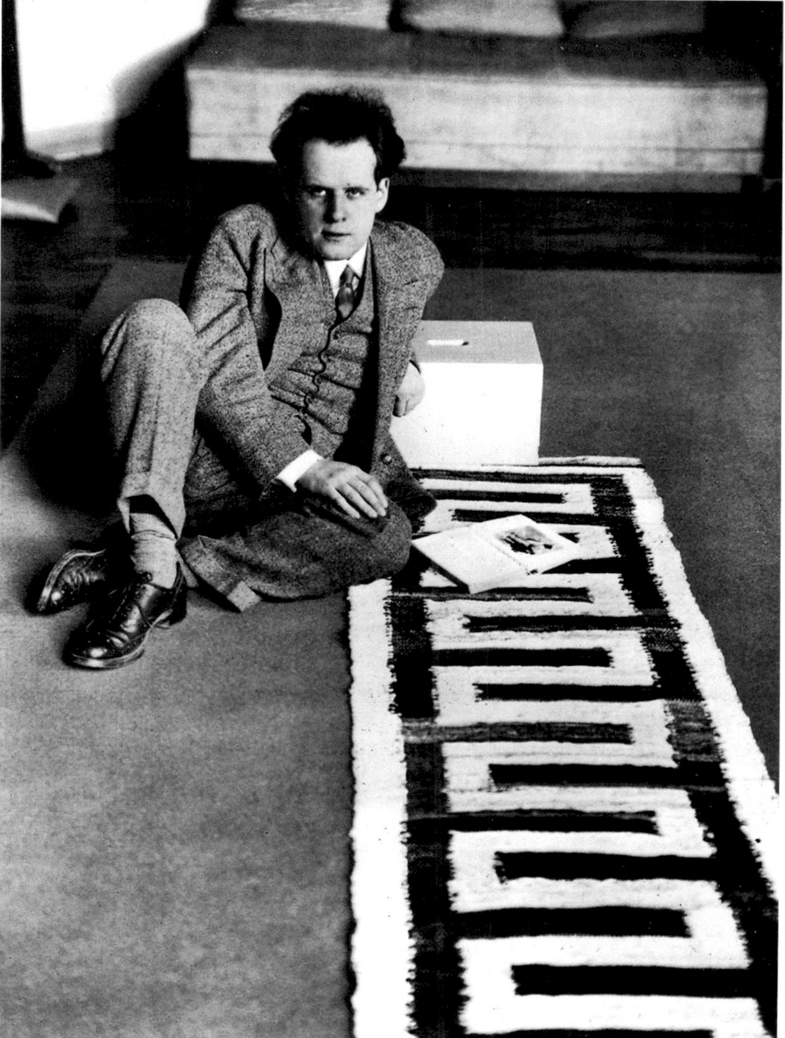

26. Colette, Paris, 1930.

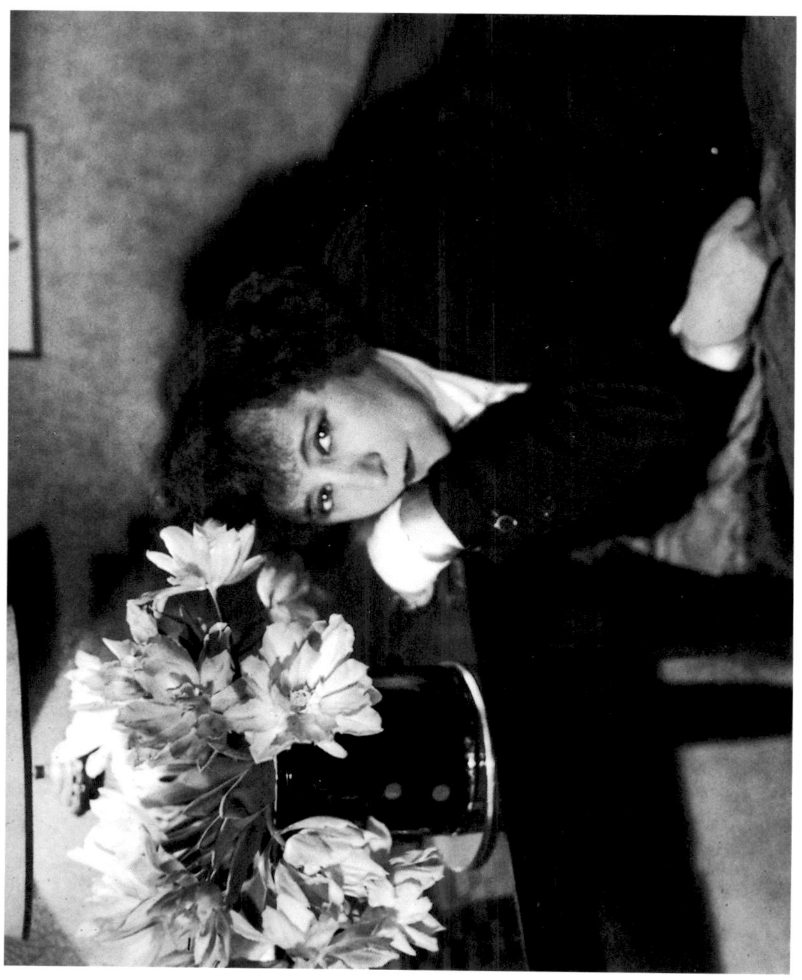

27. Melancholy tulip, New York, 1939.

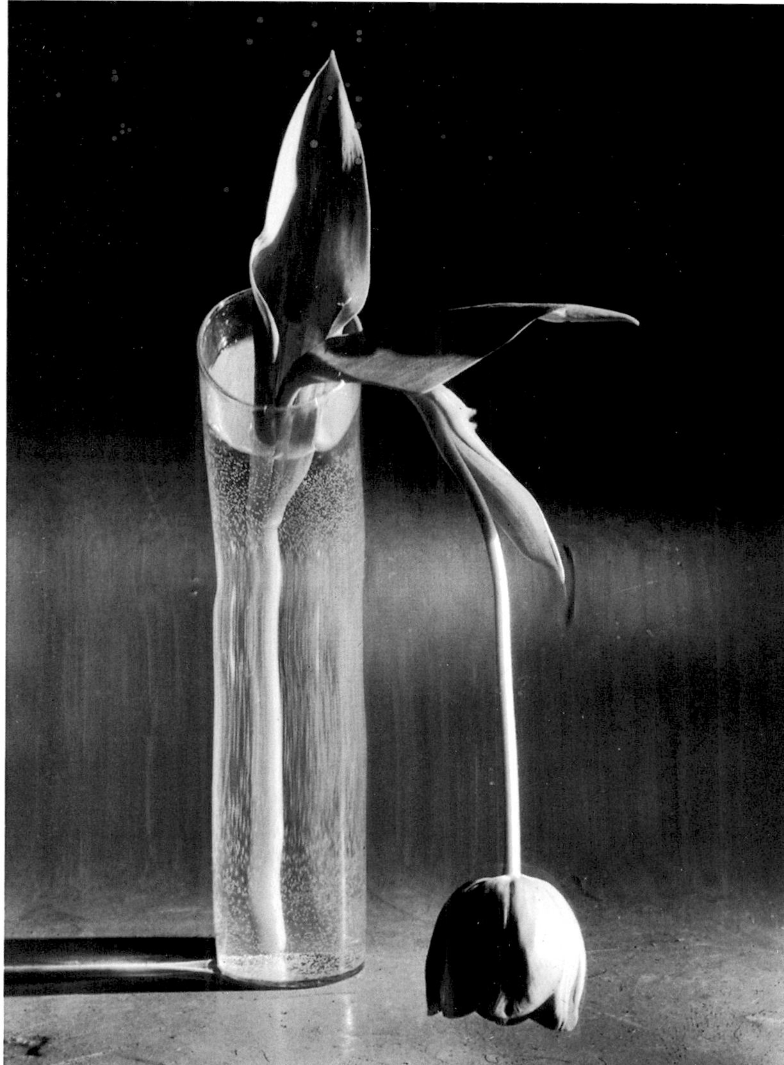

28. The Couch, Williamsburg, Virginia, 1951.

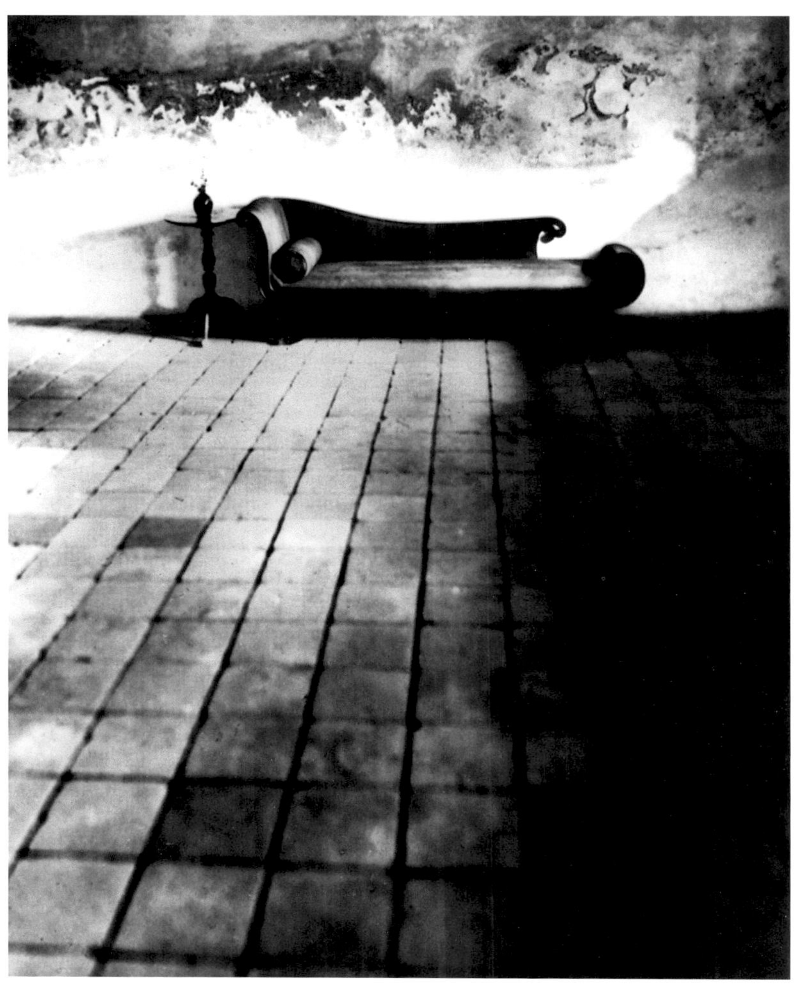

29. Museum of Natural History, New York, 1969.

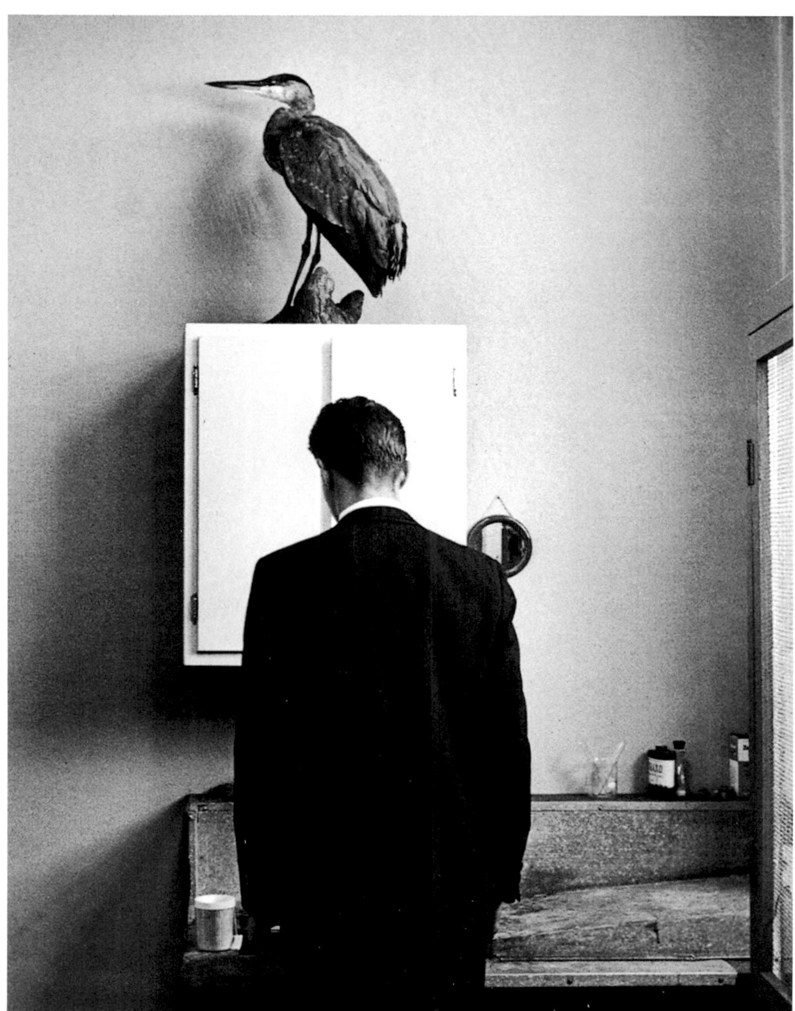

30. Elizabeth and I, Paris, 1931.

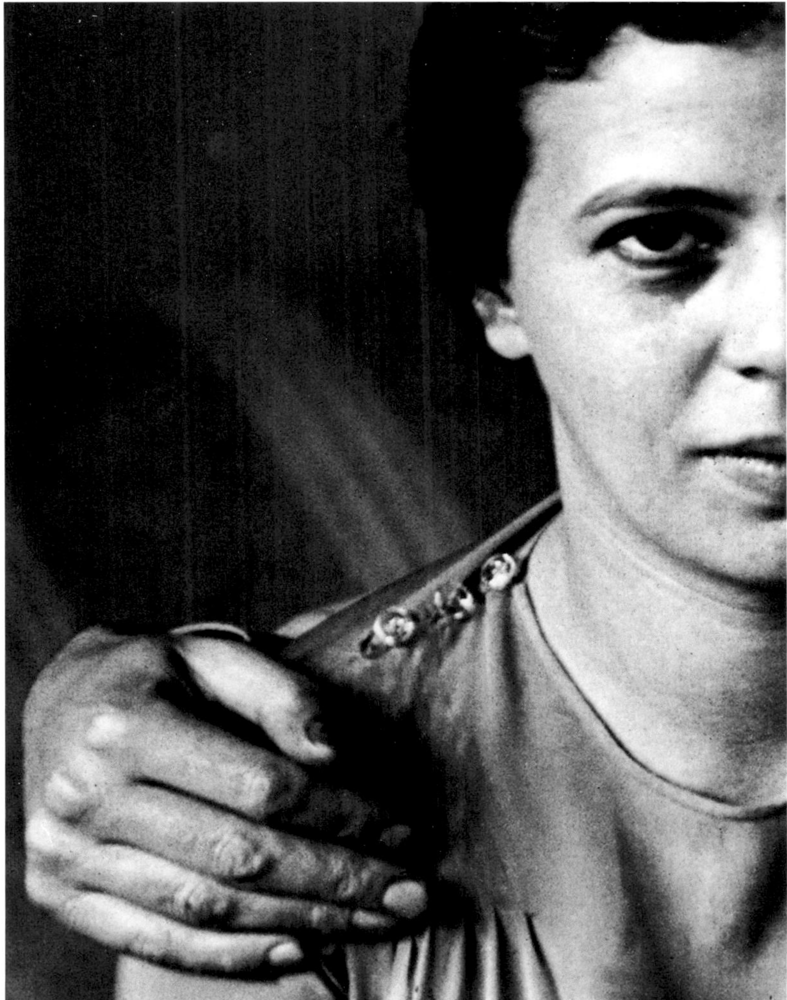

31. Bobino, Paris, 1932.

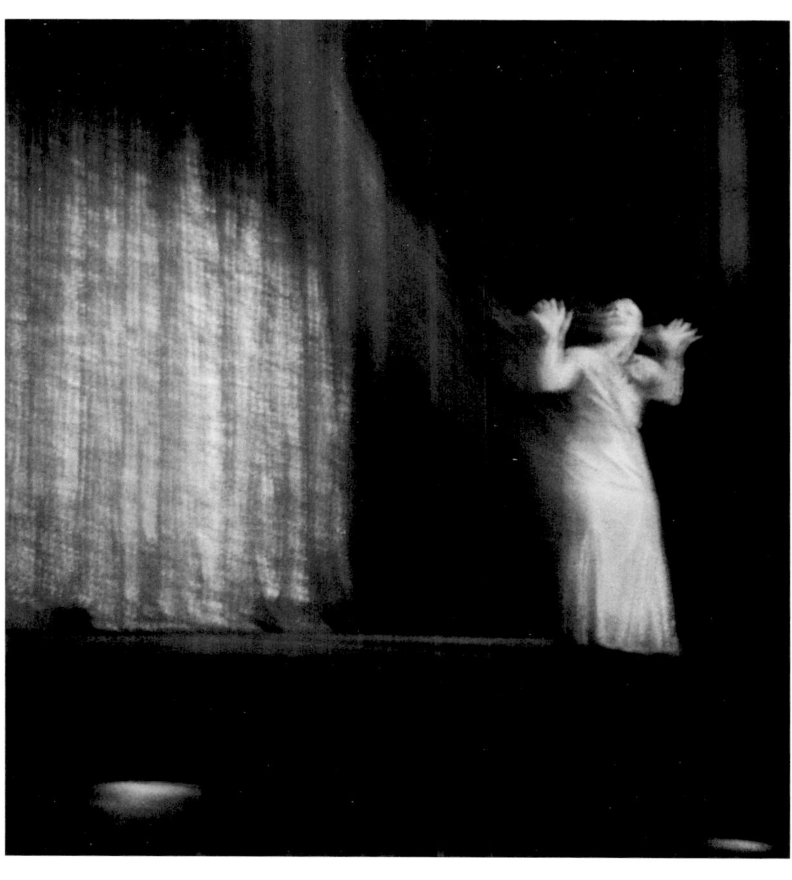

32. Charles Maurras at *Action Française*, Paris, 1928.

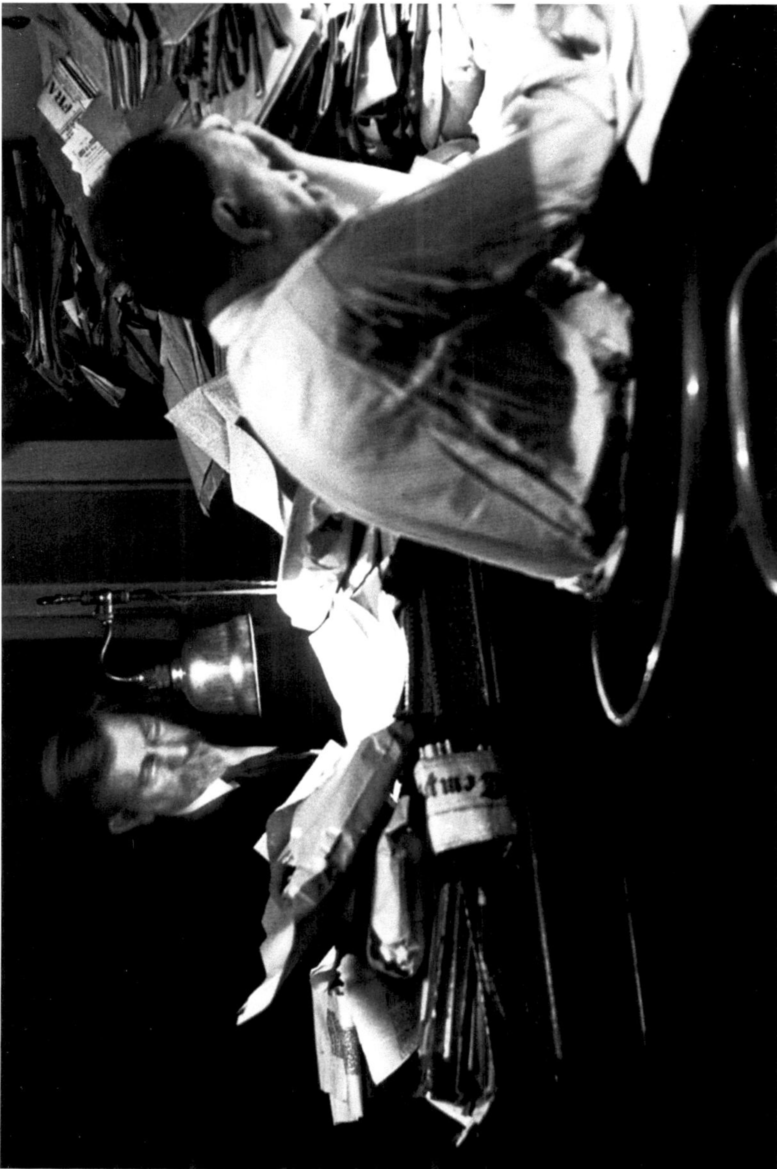

33. Meudon, France, 1928.

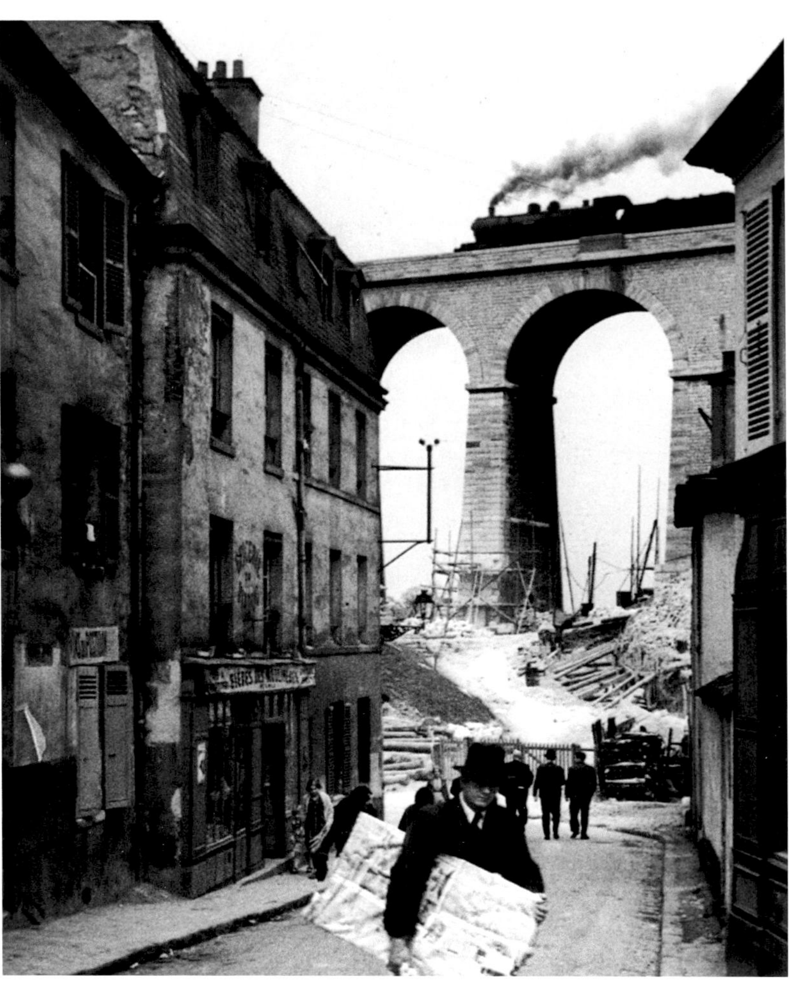

34. Outside a café, Paris, 1928.

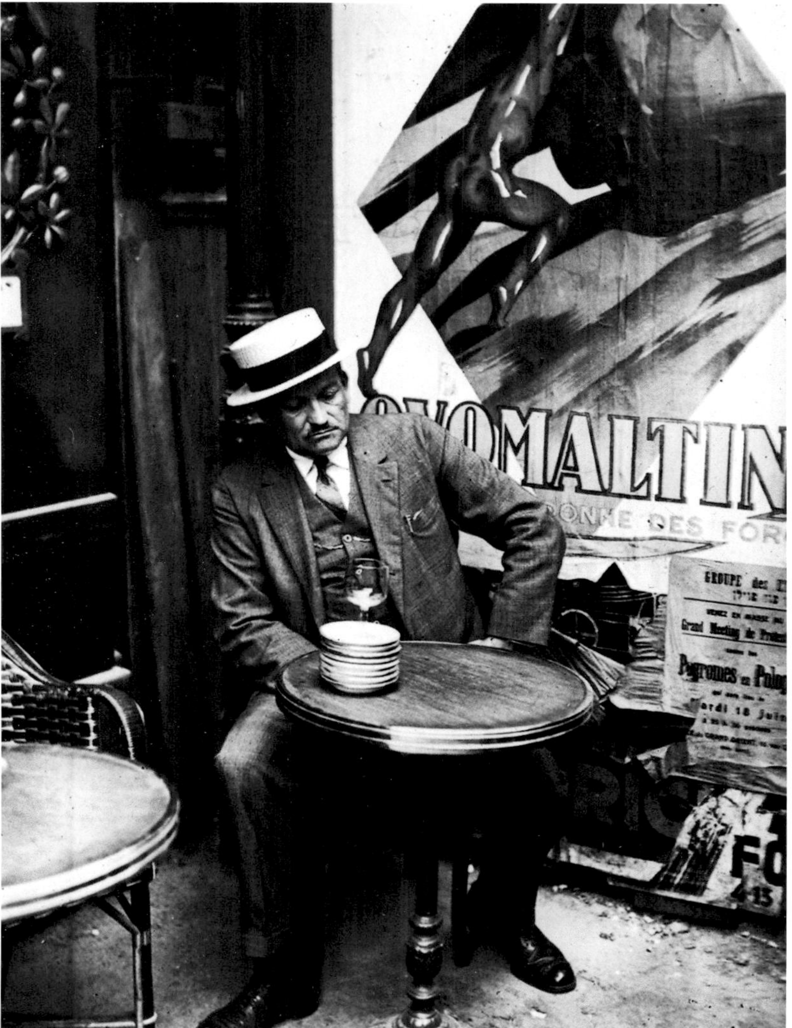
OVOMALTINE
DONNE DES FORC
GROUPE des É
Grand Meeting de Protes
Pogromes en Polog
ardi 18 juin
FO
13

35. Bonifacio, Corsica, 1932.

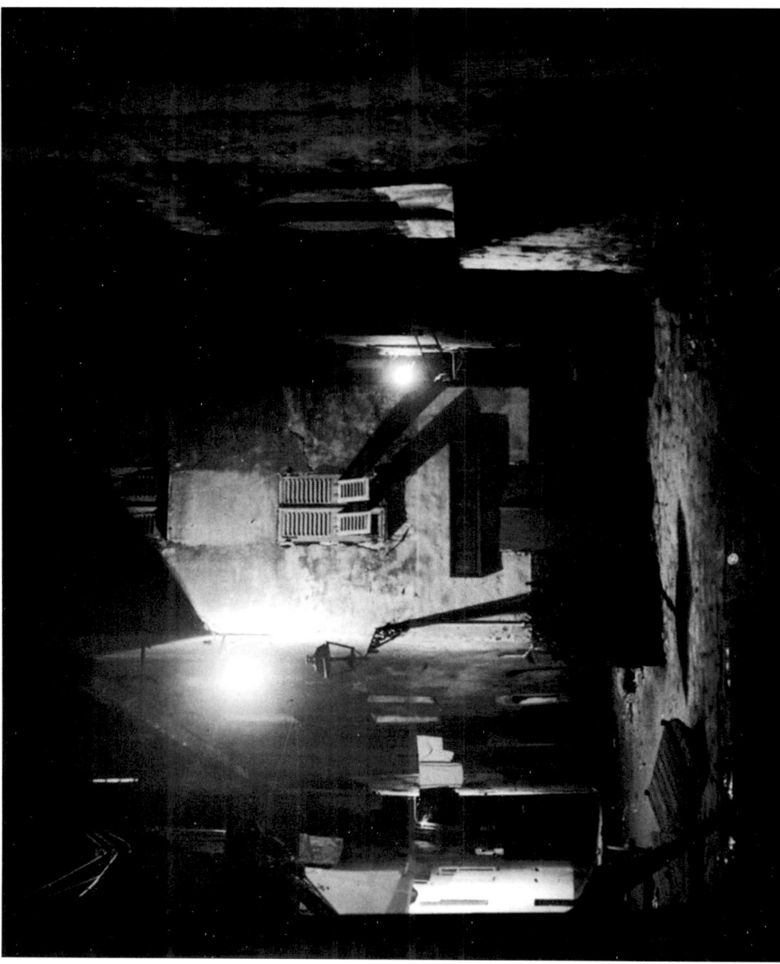

36. Dubo, Dubon, Dubonnet, Paris, 1934.

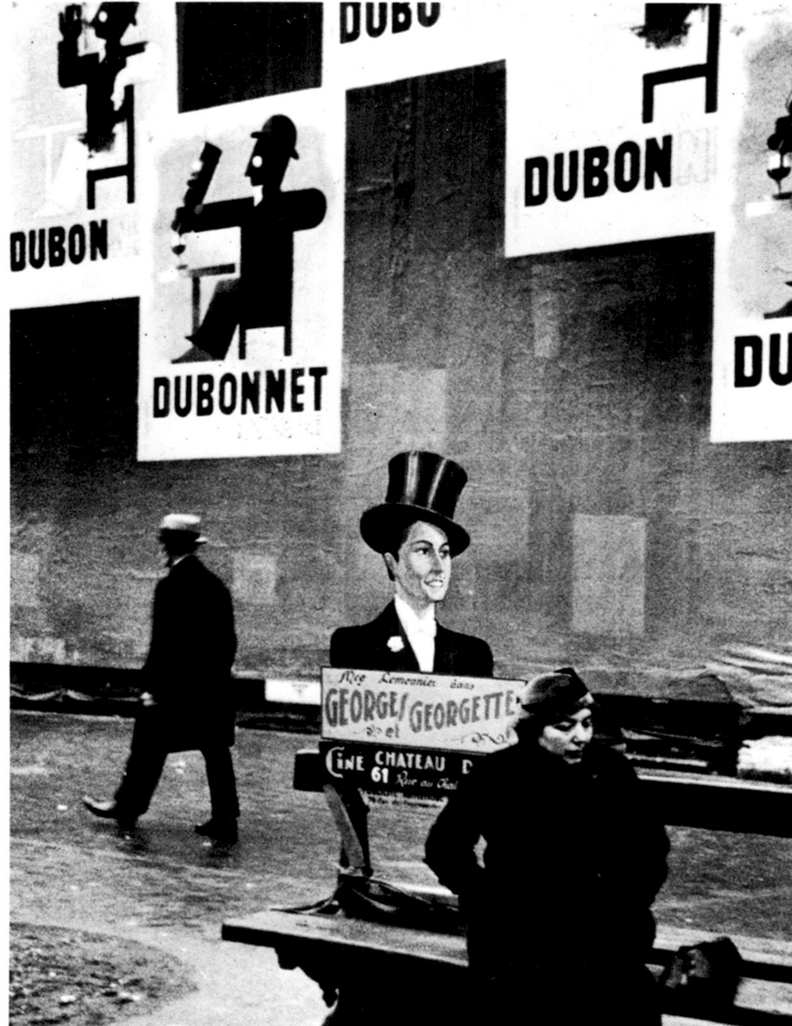

DUBO
DUBON
DUBON
DUBONNET
Meg Lemonnier dans
GEORGES et GEORGETTE
Ciné CHATEAU D
61 Rue au

37. Intersection, Blois, France, 1930.

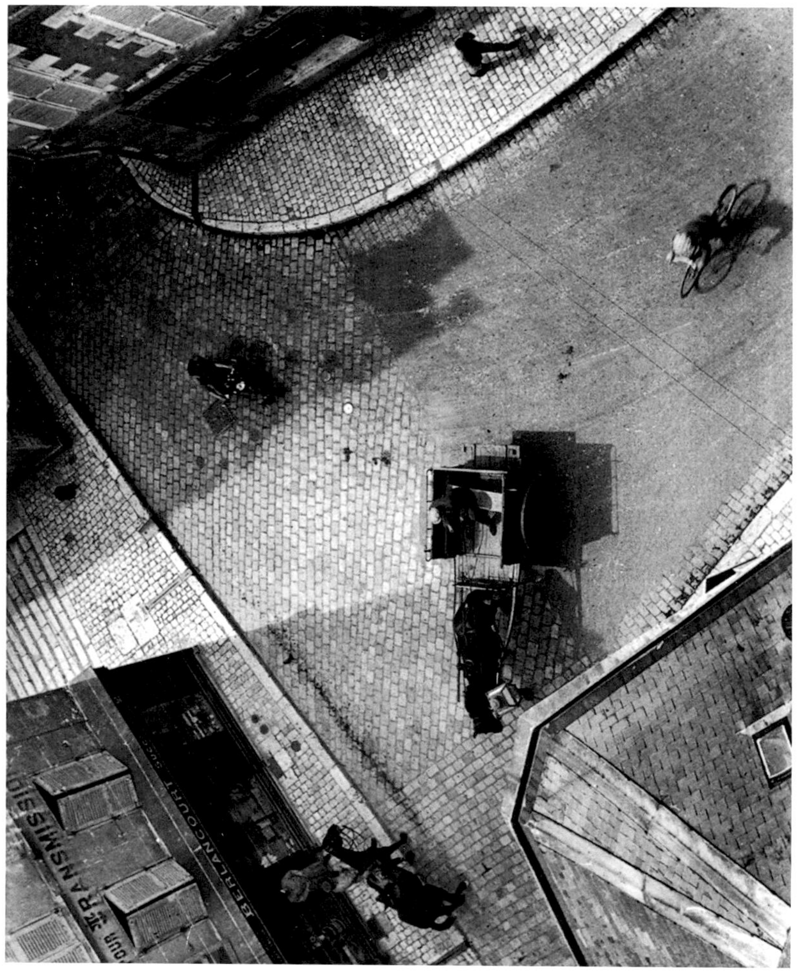

38. Street fair, Paris, 1930.

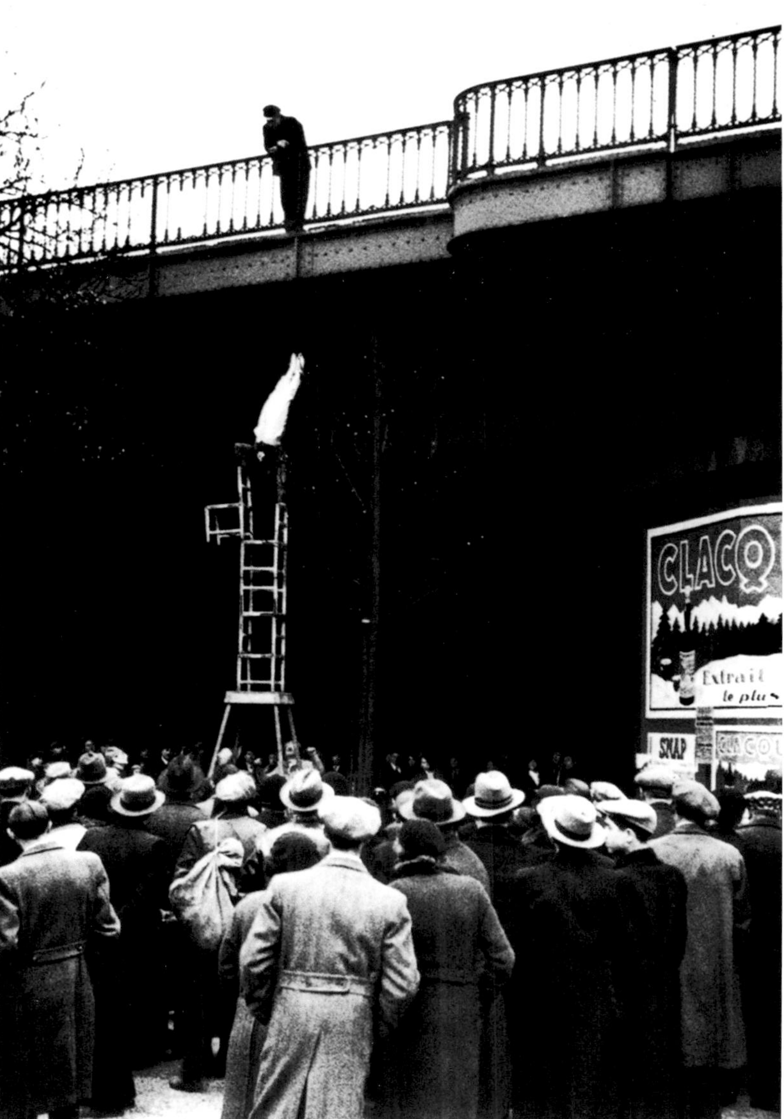

CLACQ
Extrait
le plus
SNAP

39. Istvan Rajk in a Montmartre bistro, Paris, 1931.

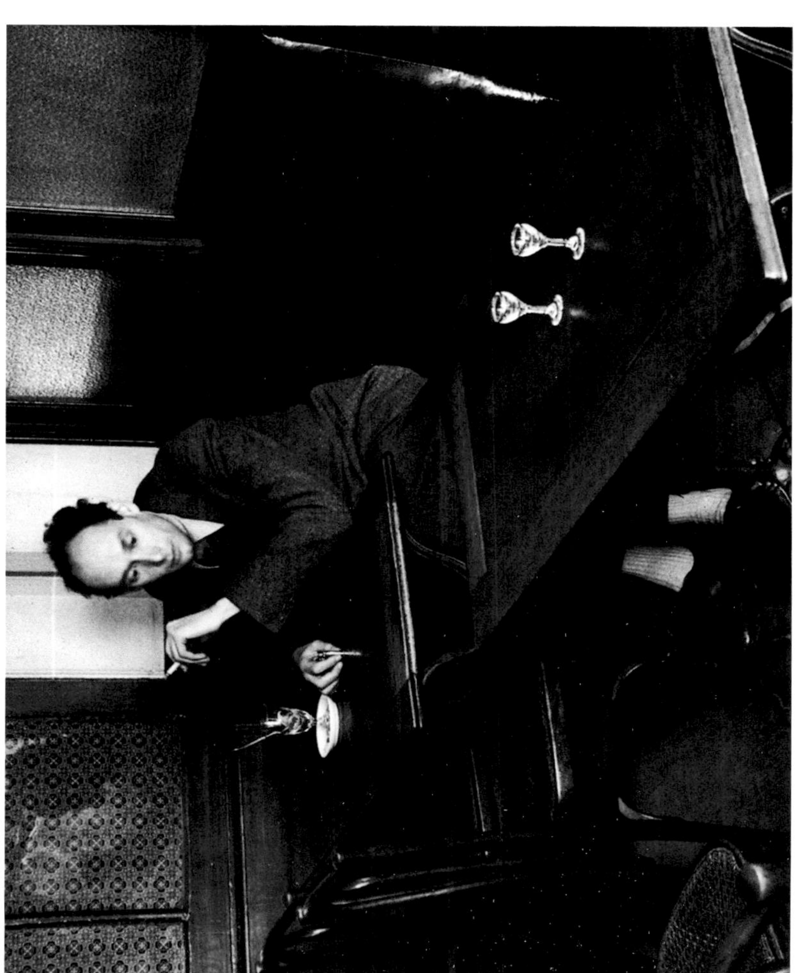

40. Shadow of the Eiffel Tower, Paris, 1929.

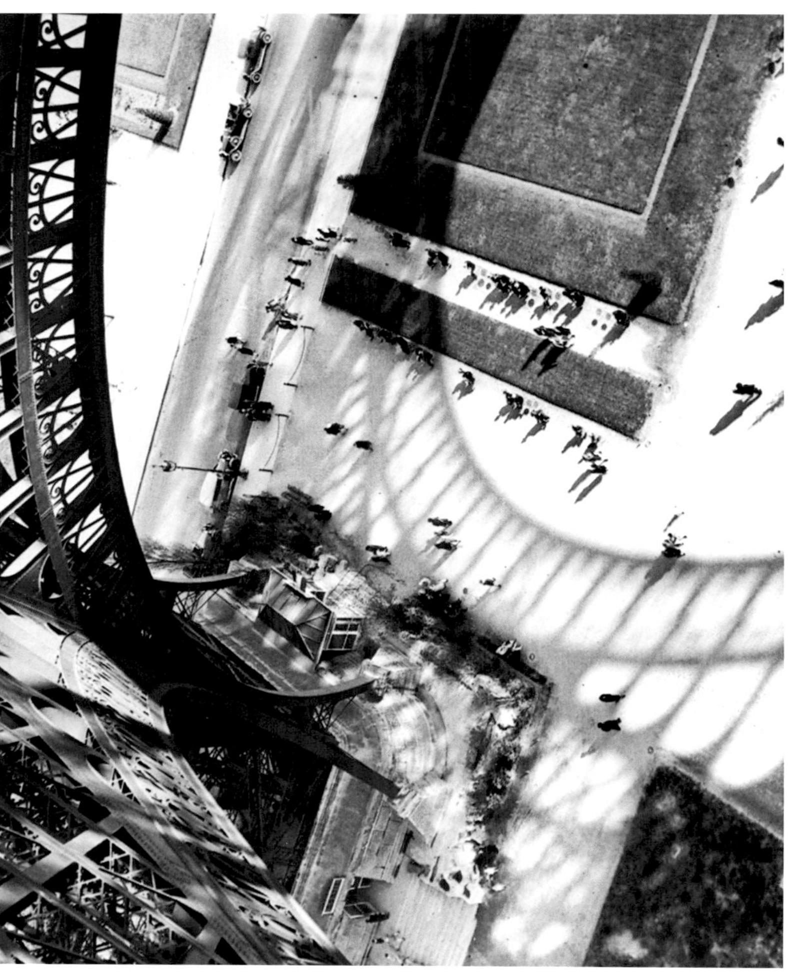

41. Versailles, 1929.

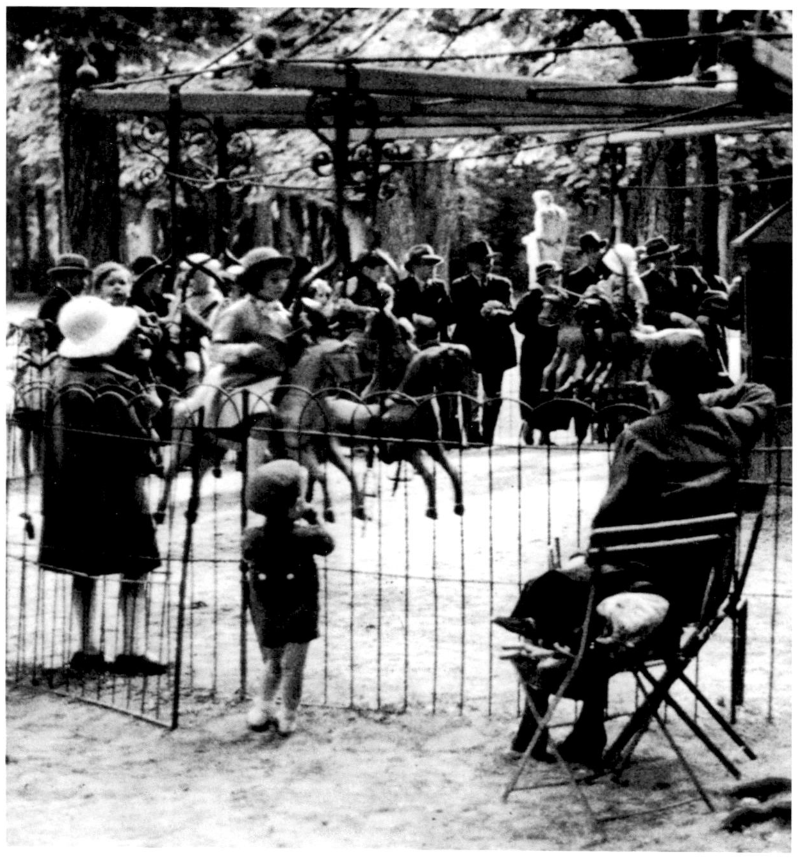

42. Luxembourg Gardens, Paris, 1928.

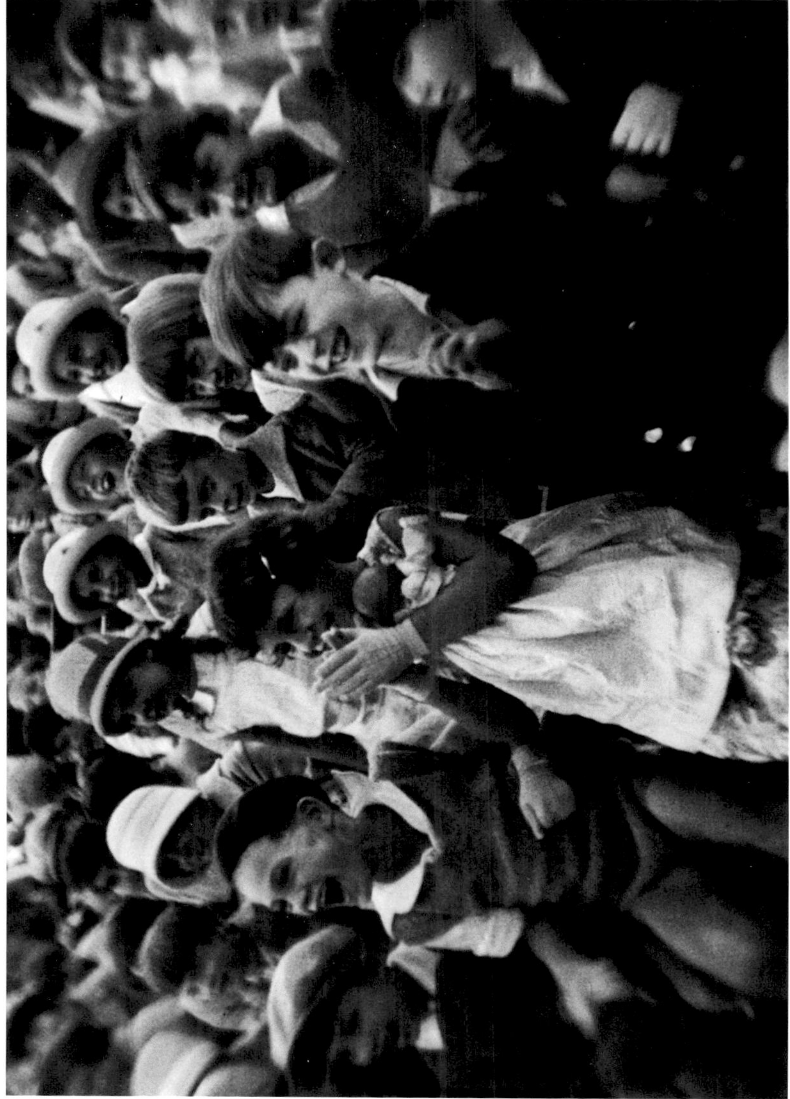

43. The boat returns home, New York, 1944.

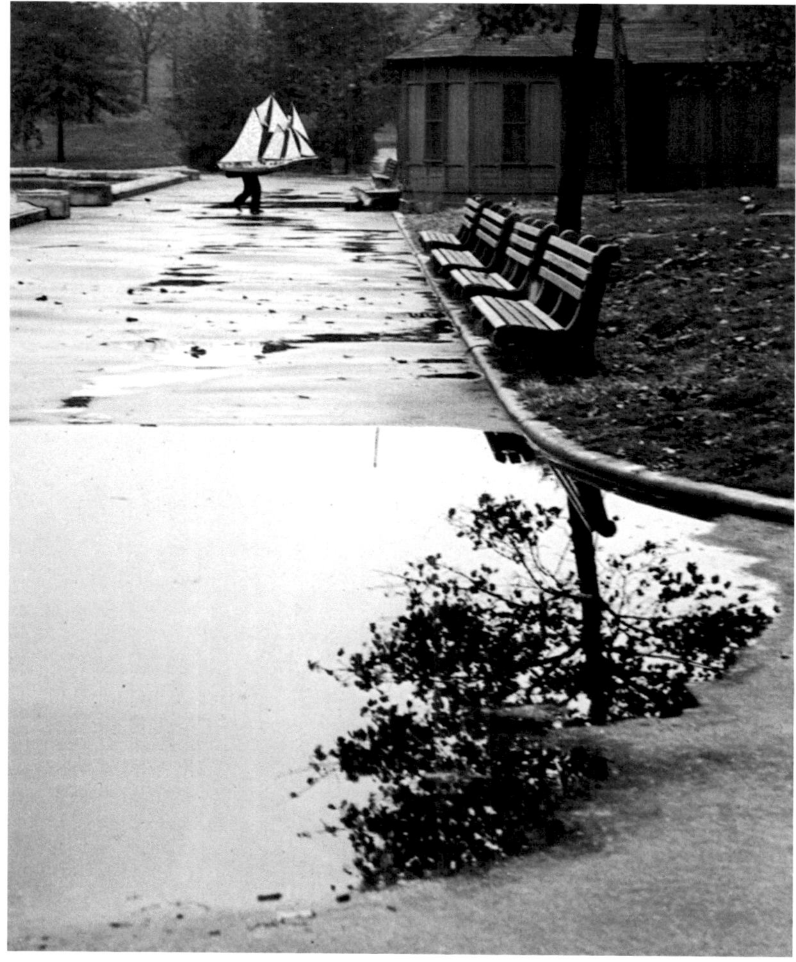

44. Street fair, 1945.

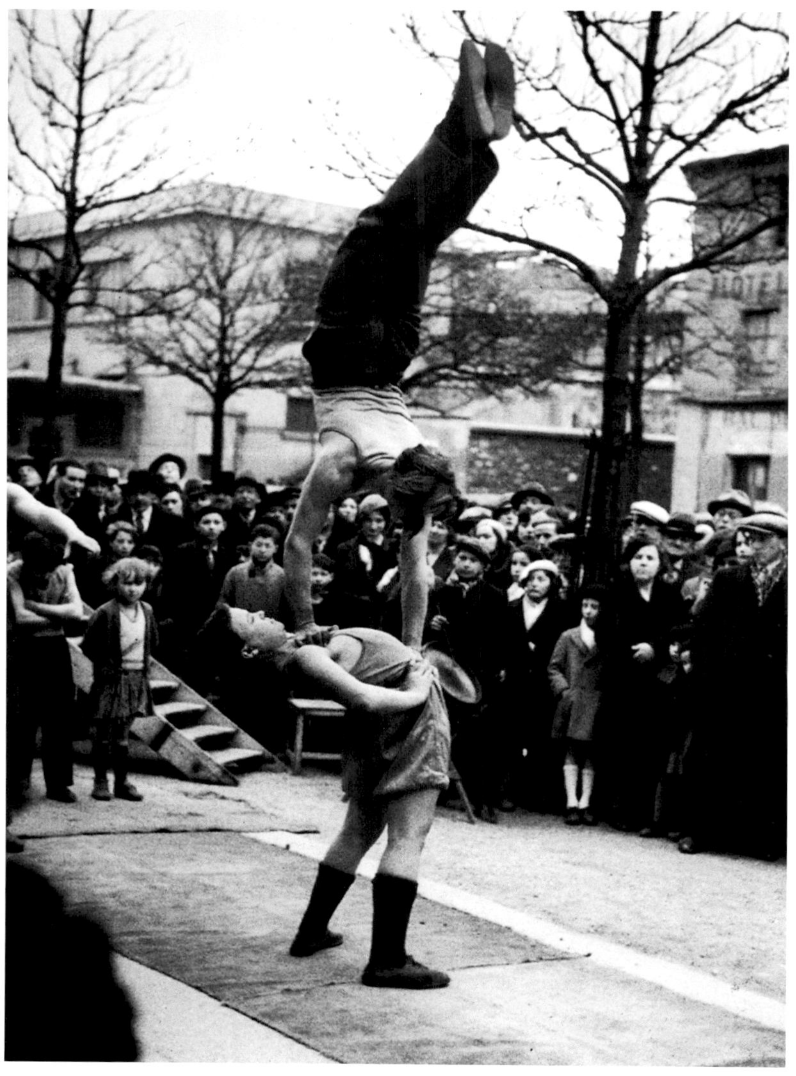

45. Paris, 1928.

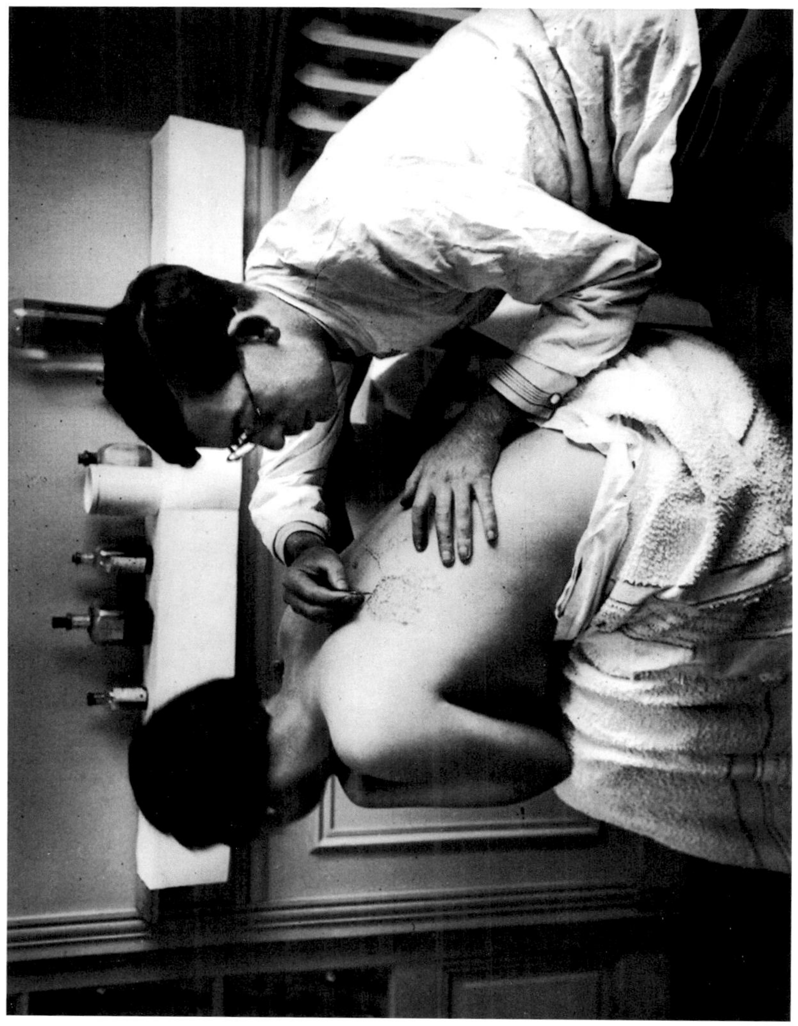

46. New York, 1947.

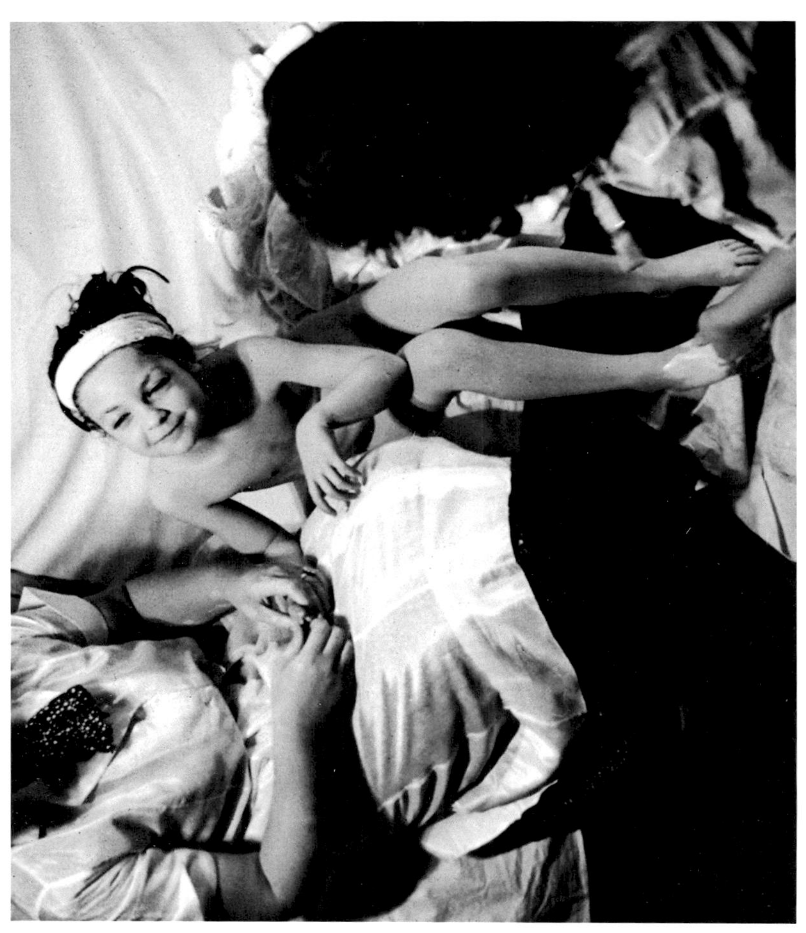

47. United States, 1953.

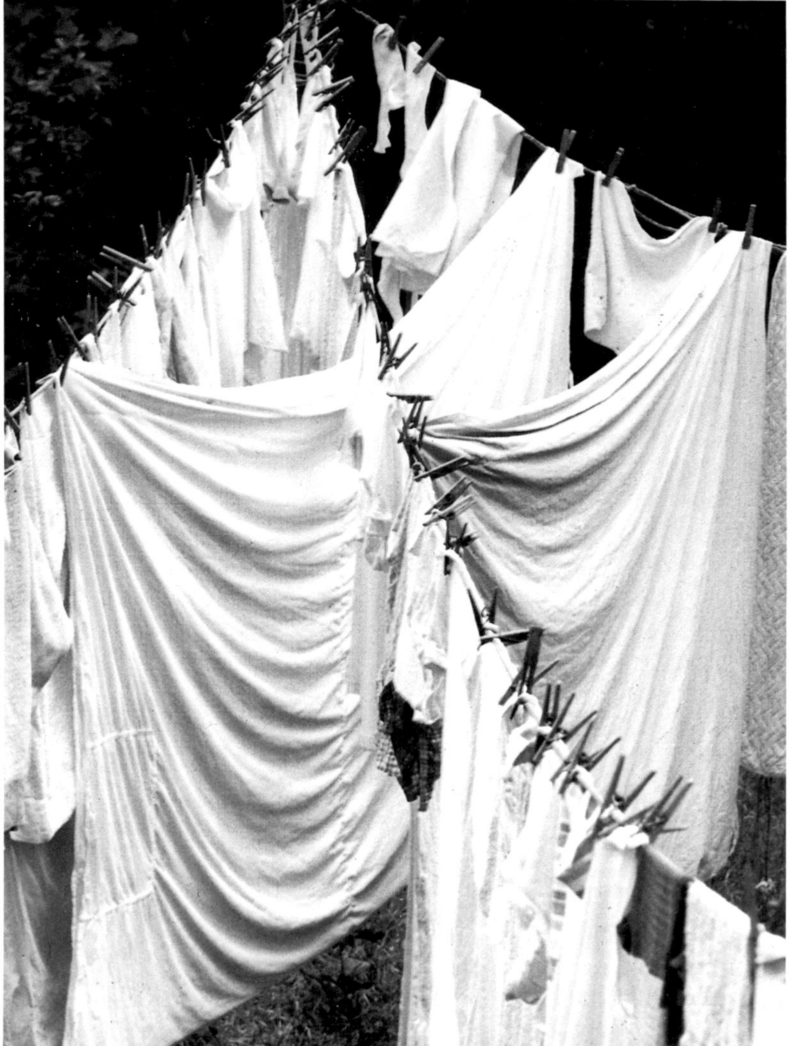

48. Overhead crosswalk with clock, New York, 1947.

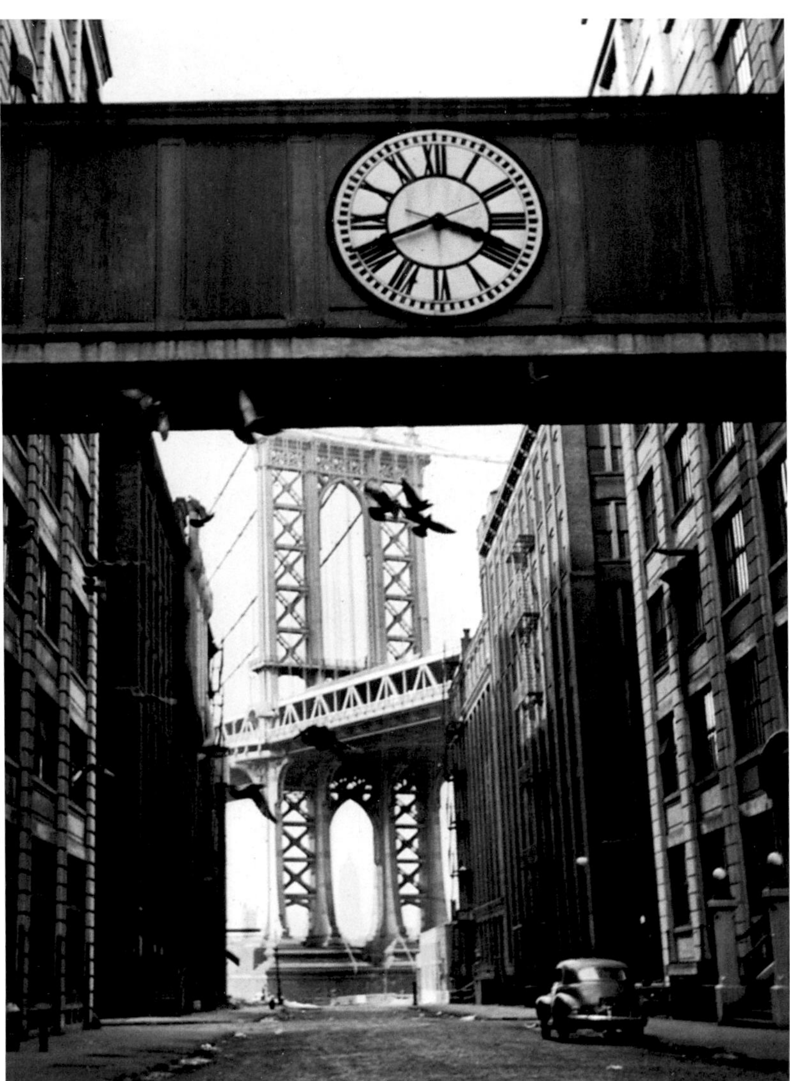

49. New York, 1971.

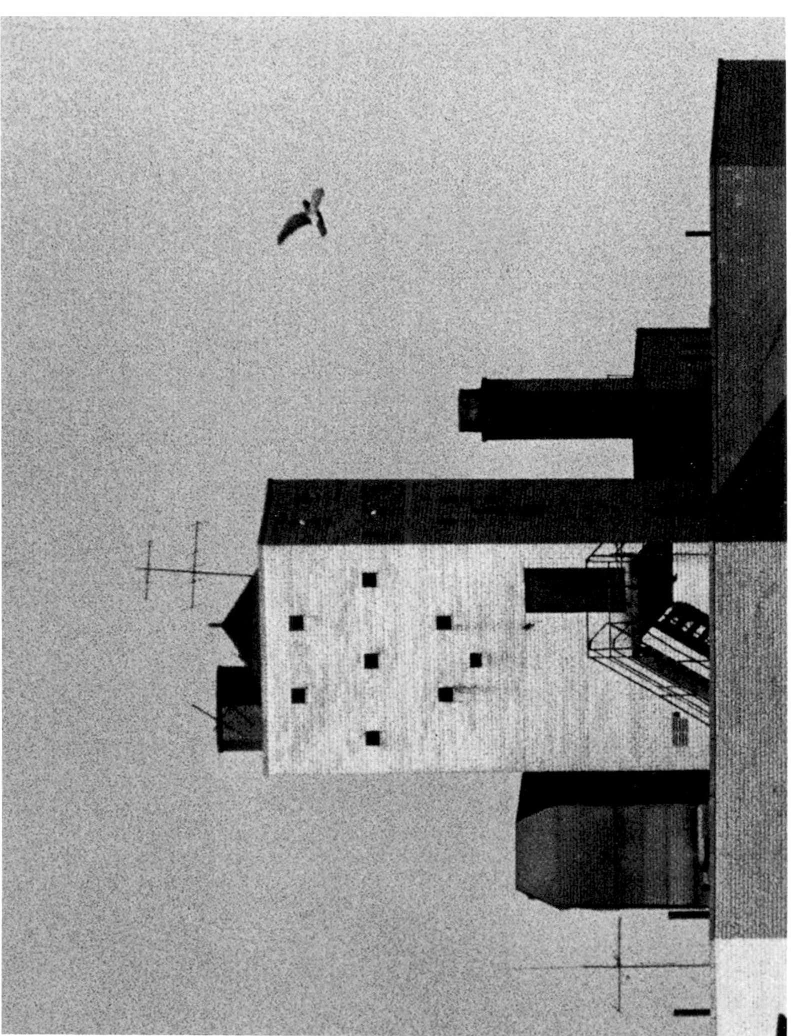

50. New York, 1973.

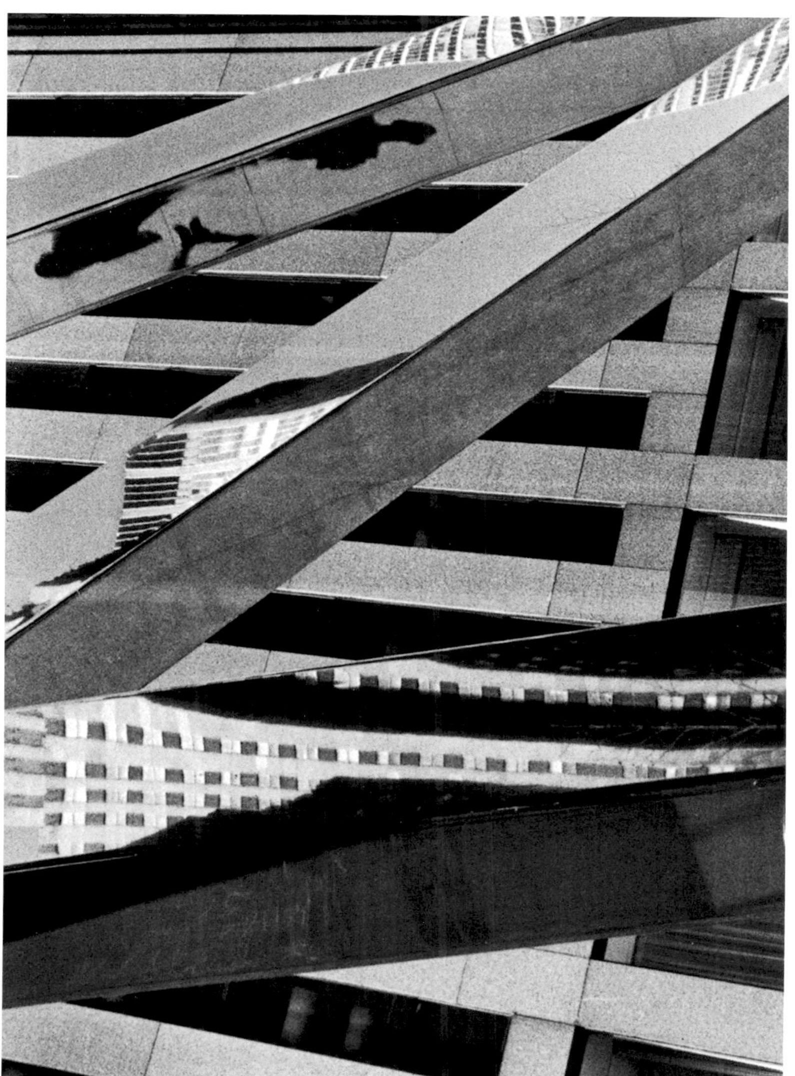

51. 'Buy', Long Island University, United States, 1962.

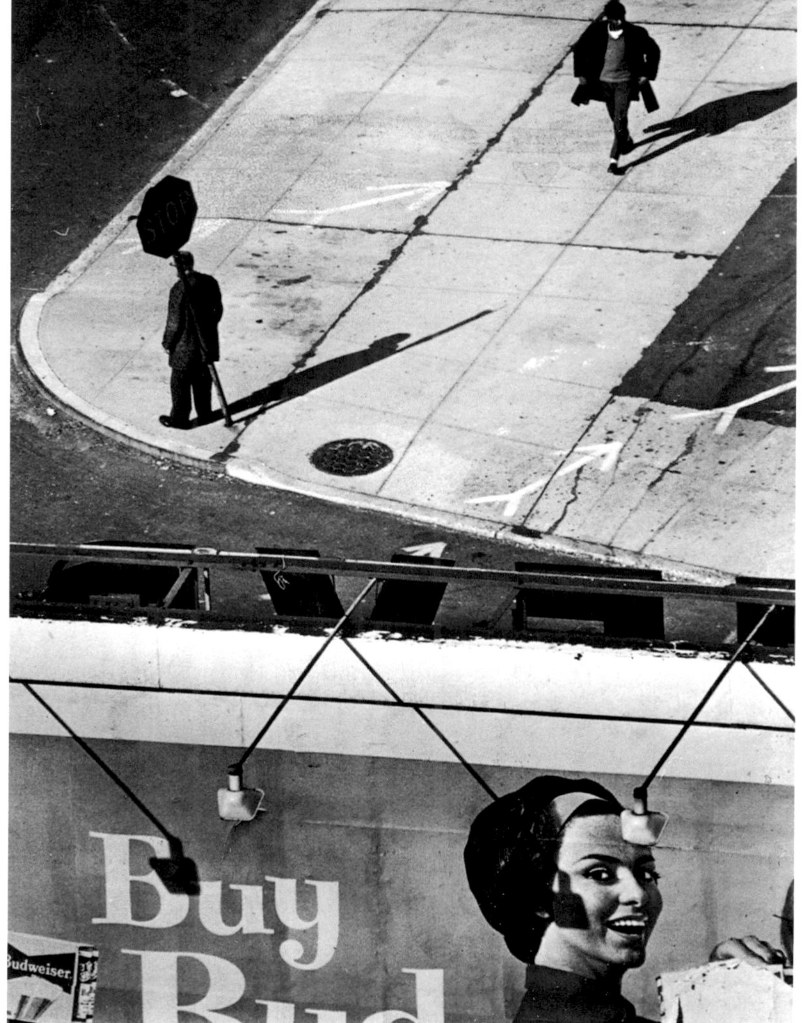

STOP
Buy
Bud
Budweiser.

52. Rainy day, Tokyo, 1968.

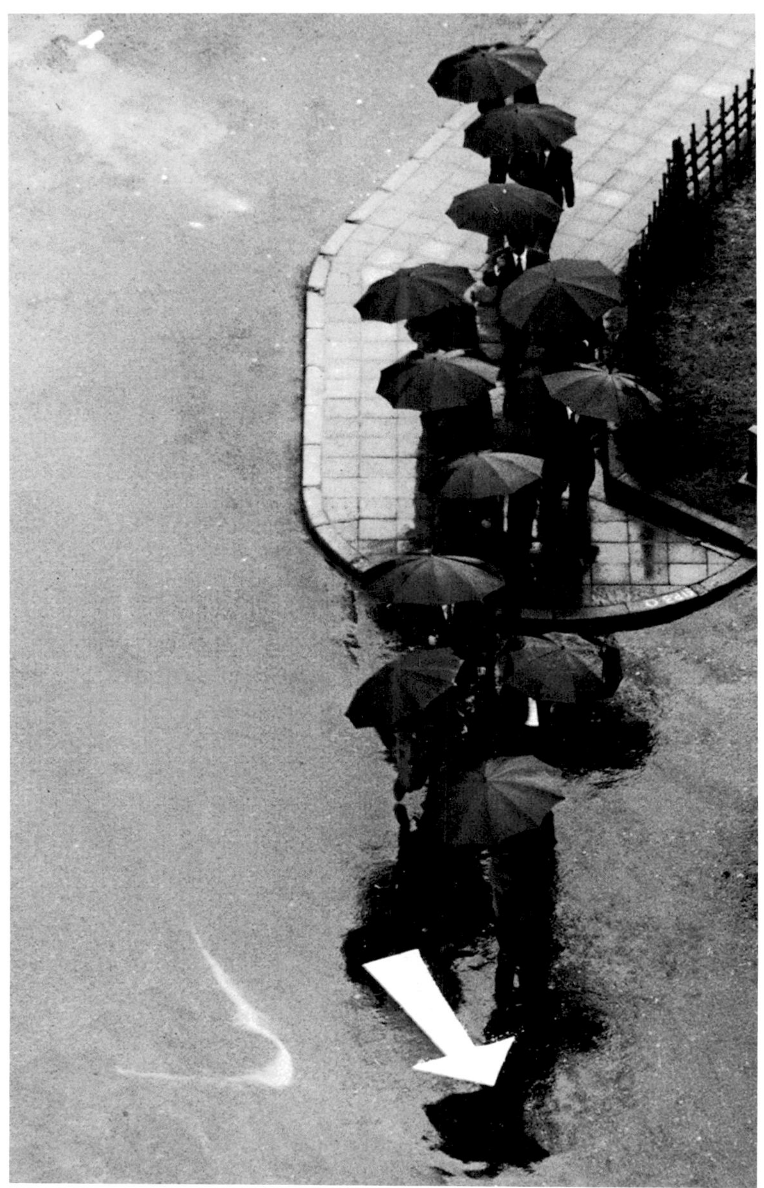

53. New York, 1960.

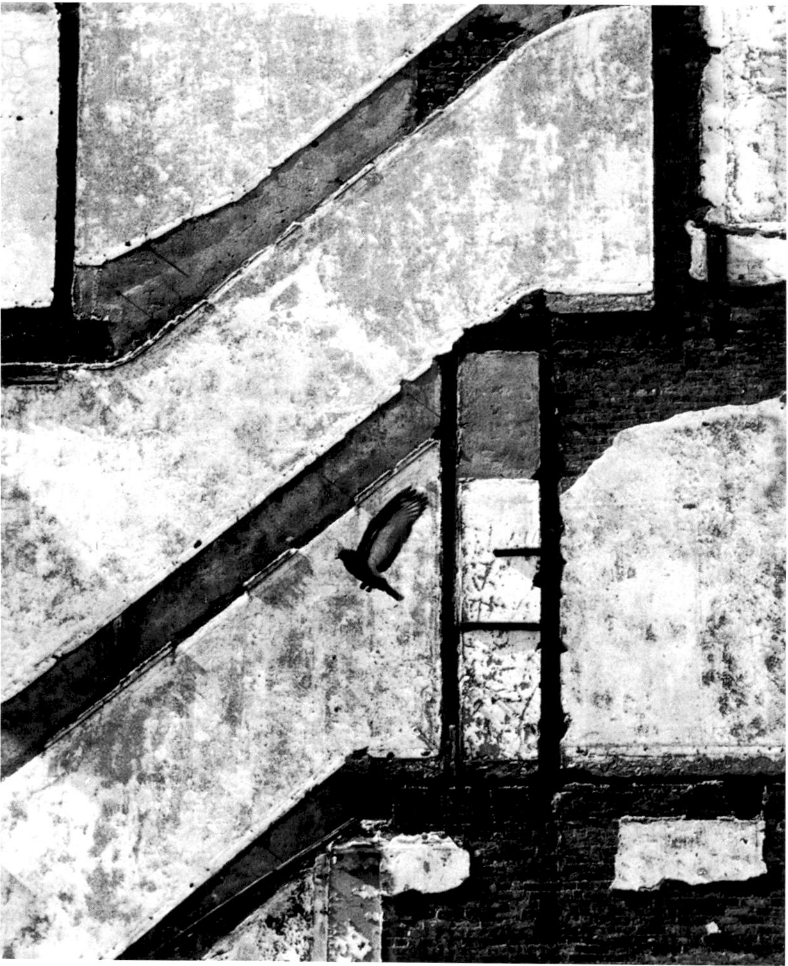

54. Winter garden, New York, 1970.

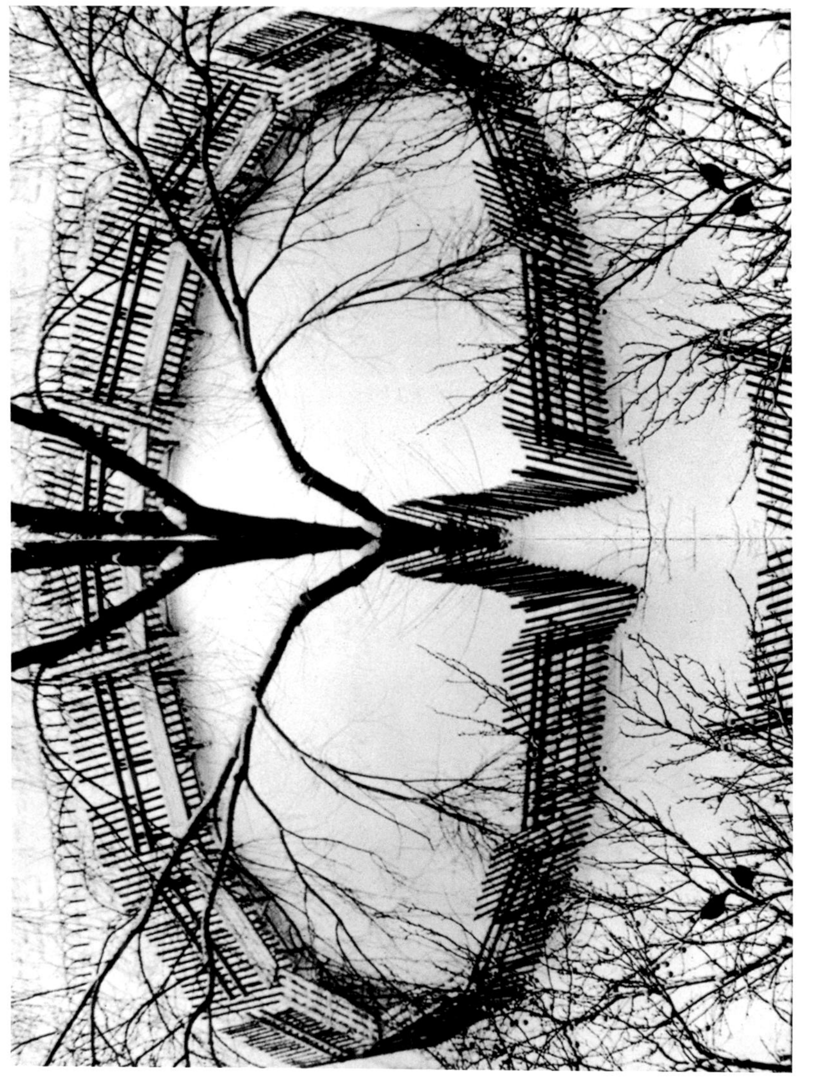

55. New York, 1970.

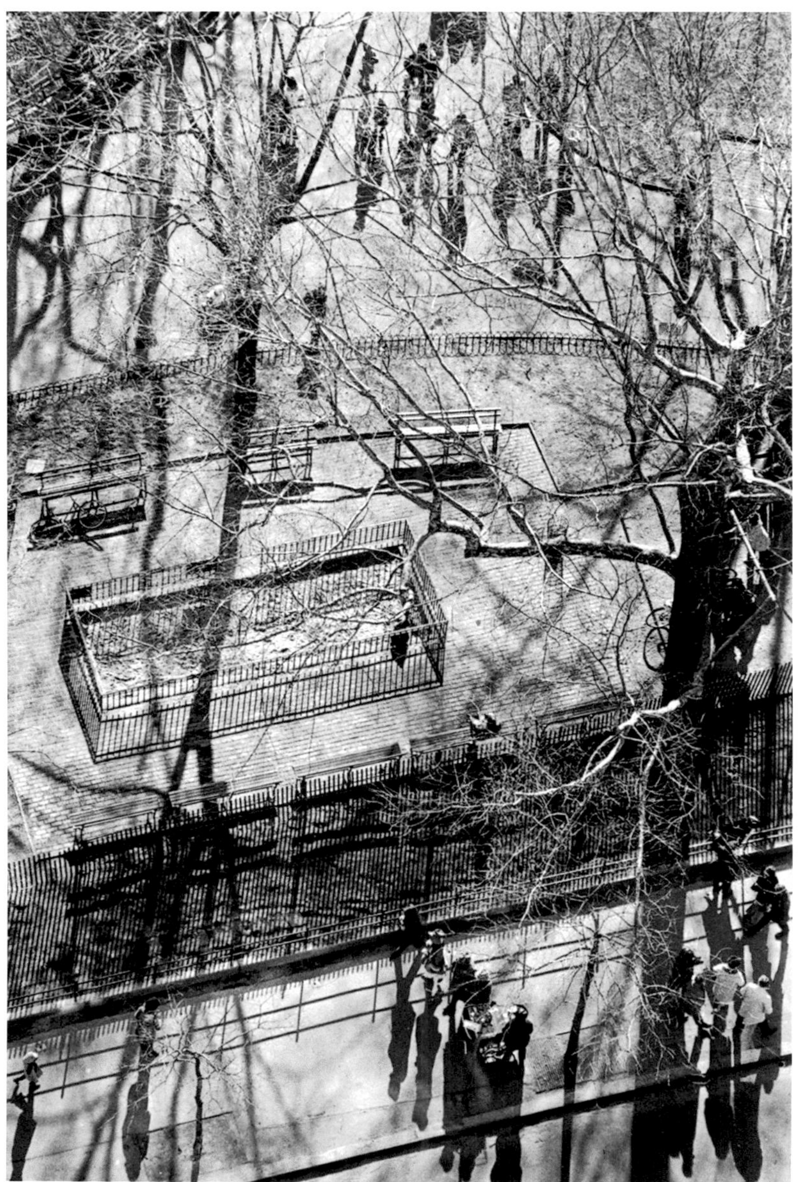

56. The disappearance, New York, 1955.

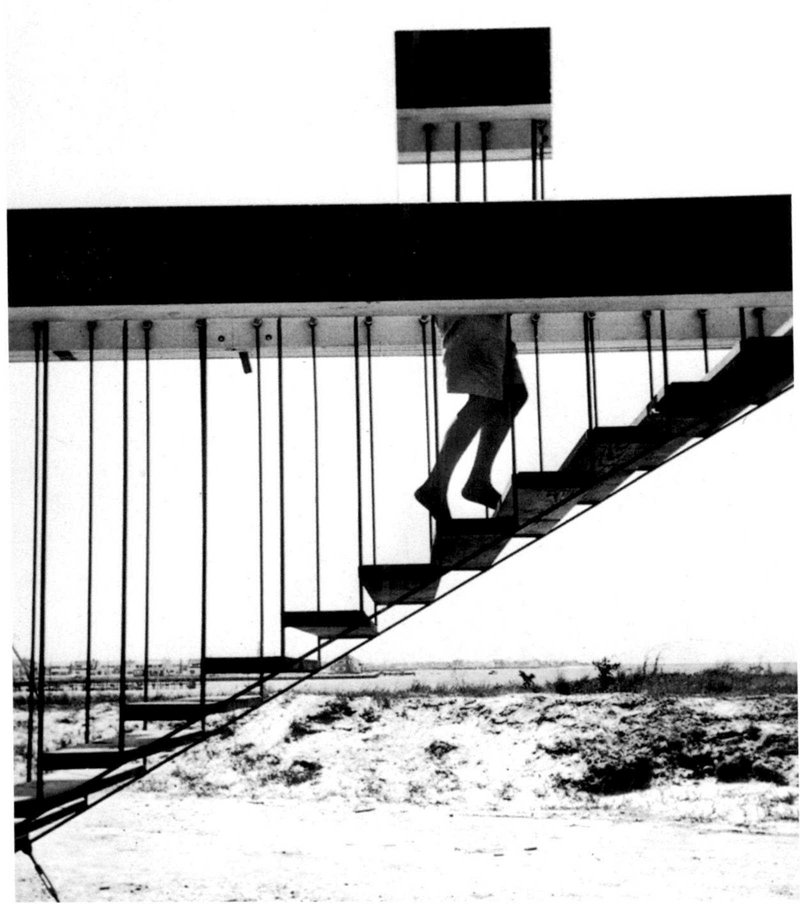

57. Underwater swimming, Hungary, 1917.

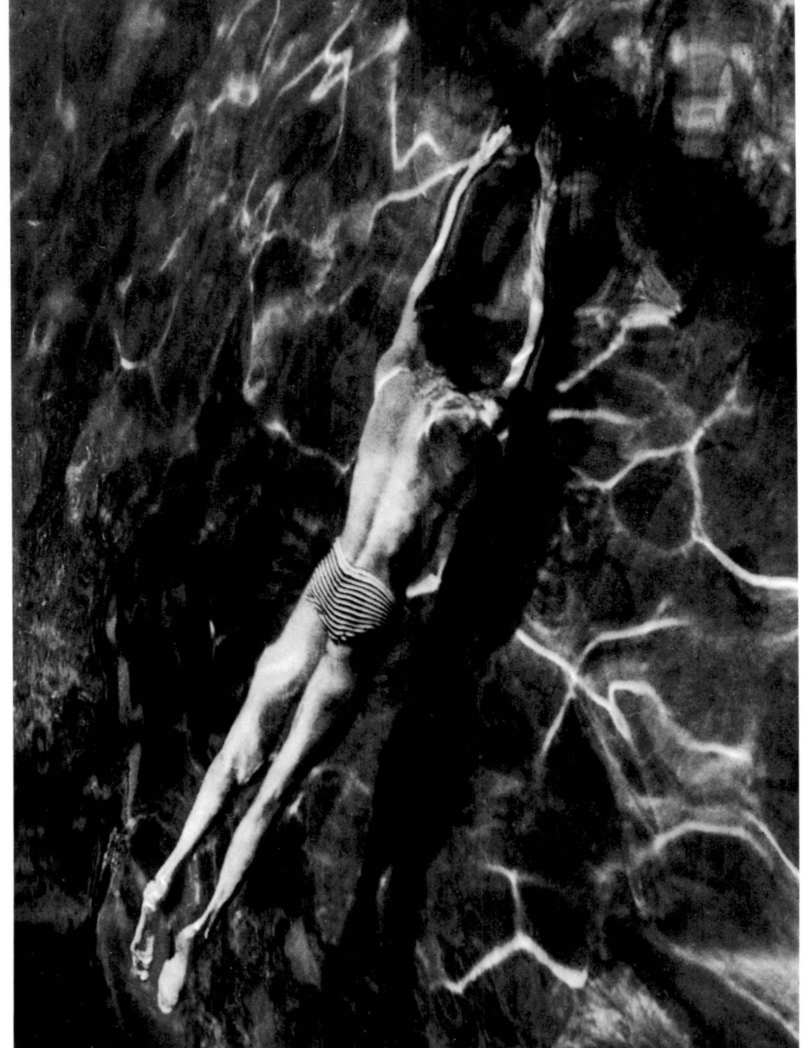

58. Martinique, 1 January 1972.

When Kertész's camera clicks,
I feel his heart beat; when he blinks,
it's a spark of Euclid, and all in an
admirable span of curiosity.

Henri Cartier-Bresson, January 1985

Biography

1894 Andor Kertész is born on 2 July in Budapest, Hungary. His businessman father dies in 1908.

1912 A graduate of the Academy of Commerce, he gets a job in the Budapest Stock Exchange. He buys his first camera (an ICA with plates, 4.5 x 6) and begins to take naive street scenes.

1914–15 Recruited by the Austro-Hungarian army in the Balkans and Central Europe, he is wounded in 1915. He takes amateur pictures of his war comrades. Many negatives from this period are lost during the 1918 revolution.

1916 He receives a prize in an amateur self-portrait competition, awarded by the satirical magazine *Borsszem Jankó*.

1917 A dozen of his photos are reproduced as postcards. He publishes pictures in the magazine *Érdekes Ujság*.

1918–25 Resumes his job at the Stock Exchange in Budapest. Photographs his family, friends and the Hungarian countryside.

1925 Like many foreign artists, André Kertész arrives in Paris and settles in Montparnasse, where he frequents the Café du Dôme, a meeting place for the avant-garde. He begins to take pictures of artists' workshops, street scenes, cafés, and Paris gardens and also takes portraits of Mondrian, Léger, Chagall, Brancusi, and Colette, among others.

1926 Settles in Paris. Meets Brassaï and Henri Cartier-Bresson.

1926–36 Works as a freelance photographer for the following newspapers and magazines:
In France: *Art et Industrie, Cahiers d'art, L'Art vivant, Ce Temps-ci, Les Annales, Voilà, L'Image, La Vie au foyer, Marianne, Regards, La France à table, Vogue, Plaisir de France, Lycéennes, Notre avenir, L'Illustré, Ève, Scandale, Votre beauté, Rails de France, Paris-Magazine, Tourisme et Santé, Les Nouvelles littéraires, L'Illustration, Le Jardin des lettres, La Mère et l'Enfant*
In Germany: *Frankfurter Illustrierte, Neue Jugend, Mode und Kultur, Das Illustrierte Blatt, Die Dame, Münchener Illustrierte, Uhu, Berliner Illustrirte Zeitung, Neueste Illustrierte*
In Britain: *The Sphere, The Sketch.*
Many portraits of Mondrian, Léger, Chagall, Zadkine, Lurçat, Calder, Brancusi, Colette, Eisenstein, Dermée, Tzara, among others.

1927 One-man show at Au Sacre du Printemps, 5 rue du Cherche-Midi, an avant-garde gallery run by Jan Slivinsky. Paul Dermée writes the foreword for the catalogue. Several photos are published by the surrealist magazine *Bifur*.

1928 Purchases his first Leica. Marries Rózsa Klein, a photographer known by the name of Rogi André. They live on the Boulevard Montparnasse in Paris but separate two years later.

1928–35 *Vu*, the magazine edited by Lucien Vogel, begins publication, and Kertész makes many contributions to it.

1929 He exhibits at the *Film und Foto* exhibition in Stuttgart, organized by the German Werkbund, and at the *Contemporary Photography* exhibition in Essen, which brings together many avant-garde photographers. His photos are bought by the Berlin Staatliche Museum Kunstbibliothek and the König-Albert Museum in Zwickau.

1930 Works alongside Brassaï, Kollar, Sougez, Krull and May Ray on the magazine *Art et Médecine* until 1936.

1932 He exhibits 35 prints at the *Modern European Photography* show at the Julien Levy Gallery in New York.

1933 He produces the famous distortion series published by the magazine *Le Sourire*, using a distorting mirror, a Linhof chamber and a combination of lenses. He marries Elizabeth Sali.

1934 Publication of *Paris vu par André Kertész*, with an introduction by Pierre MacOrlan.

1936 Ernie Prince, director of the Keystone Agency, invites Kertész and his wife to New York in October and gives Kertész a contract which he breaks the following year. The Second World War prevents him from returning to Europe.

1937–49 Freelance fashion and interior photographer for *Harper's Bazaar*, *Vogue*, *Town and Country*, *The American Magazine*, *Collier's*, *Coronet* and *Look*.

1941 Prevented from publication for several years due to his nationality. The Museum of Modern Art in New York becomes the first US museum to buy one of his photographs, for the exhibition *Image of Freedom*.

1944 Becomes an American citizen.

1945 Publication of *Day of Paris*, designed by Alexey Brodovitch.

1946 First US solo exhibition at the Chicago Art Institute.

1949–62 Signs an exclusivity contract with Condé Nast Publications.

1952 Moves to 5th Avenue, New York. Begins a series of photographs of Washington Square that will become a lifelong personal project, and are the subject of a book in 1975.

c. 1955 First colour photographs.

1963 Recovers the negatives from his Hungarian and French periods, which were hidden in a chateau in the south of France during the war. Wins a gold medal at the 4th International Photography Biennale of Venice. One-man show at the Bibliothèque Nationale de Paris. He devotes himself to creative personal photography.

1964 Solo show at the Museum of Modern Art in New York, organized by John Szarkowski.

1965–76 Takes part in several exhibitions in New York, Tokyo, Stockholm, Budapest, London and Helsinki. Receives honours from the American Society of Magazine Photographers (1965), a Guggenheim Fellowship (1974) and is named Commandeur des Arts et Belles-Lettres by the French government (1976). Continues to photograph New York from his own window.

1975 Guest of honour at the Rencontres Internationales de Photographie, Arles. Travels frequently to France until 1984.

1977 Death of Elizabeth in October.

1977–78 Major retrospective organized by the Centre Georges Pompidou, Paris, directed by Pierre de Fenoÿl.

1979–81 Takes a series of Polaroid still lifes at his New York apartment, published as *From My Window*.

1981 Given the Mayor's Award of Honor for Arts and Culture, New York.

1982 Awarded the Grand Prix National de la Photographie, Paris.

1983 Receives the Légion d'Honneur.

1984 On 30 March, signs over his personal archive of negatives and documents to the French state (Ministry of Culture). Travels to Budapest for the last time, for the Spring Festival.

1985 The exhibition *André Kertész of Paris and New York* is held at the Art Institute of Chicago and the Metropolitan Museum of Art, New York. André Kertész dies 28 September at his New York home.

1987 The André Kertész bequest arrives in Paris. The French Association of Photographic Heritage takes charge of its conservation and distribution.

1994 The André Kertész Memorial Museum officially opens on 9 April in Szigetbecse, Hungary.

Bibliography

compiled by Stuart Alexander

Publications

Enfants, text by Jaboune (pseudonym of Jean
Nohain). 60 photos. Editions d'histoire et
d'art, Librairie Plon, Paris, 1933

Paris, vu par André Kertész, text by Pierre
MacOrlan, 48 photos. Editions d'histoire et
d'art, Librairie Plon, Paris, 1934

Nos amies les bêtes, text by Jaboune,
60 photos, Editions d'histoire et d'art,
Librairie Plon, Paris, 1936

Les Cathédrales du Vin, text by Pierre Hamp,
28 photos. Etablissements Sainrapt et Brice,
Paris, 1937

Day of Paris, edited by George Davis,
102 photos. J.J. Augustin Publishers,
New York, 1945

André Kertész, introduction by Anna Fárová,
adapted for the US edition by Robert Sagalyn,
73 photos. Paragraphic Books, a division of
Grossman Publishing, New York, 1966

'André Kertész', pp. 66–91, 184–190, in *The
Concerned Photographer*, edited by Cornell
Capa, 32 photos by Kertész. Grossman
Publishers, New York, 1968. Biography,
bibliography, and commentary by Kertész

On Reading, New York, Grossman Publishers;
Lectures, Editions du Chêne, Paris, 2nd
edition, 1975. 66 photos. Reprint: Viking Press,
New York, 1982

*André Kertész: Sixty Years of Photography,
1912–1972*, edited by Nicolas Ducrot, New
York, Grossman Publishers; *André Kertész
: Soixante ans de photographies, 1912–1972*,
Editions du Chêne, 1972. 2nd edition, 1978.
235 photos, with Paul Dermée's text, 'Brother
Seeing-Eye'. Chronology, bibliography

J'aime Paris: Photographs since the Twenties,
edited by Nicolas Ducrot, 218 photos from
1925–35 and 1963. Grossman Publishers, New
York, 1974

André Kertész: Washington Square, edited
by Nicolas Ducrot, text by Brendan Gill. 103
photos. Grossman Publishers, New York, 1975

Of New York..., edited by Nicolas Ducrot, Alfred
A. Knopf, New York; *Dans New York*, Editions
du Chêne, Paris, 1976. 189 photos

Distortions, edited by Nicolas Ducrot,
introduction by Hilton Kramer, Alfred A.
Knopf, New York; *Distorsions*, Editions du
Chêne, Paris, 1976. 126 photos

André Kertész, introduction by Carole Kismaric,
Aperture History of Photography series, no.
6, Aperture, Millerton, New York; Nouvel
Observateur/Delpire, Paris, 1977. 43 photos,
chronology, bibliography. Reprint: Aperture,
New York, 1997

Americana, Birds, Landscapes, Portraits, edited
by Nicolas Ducrot, Mayflower Books, New
York, 1979; *Americana, Oiseaux, Paysages,
Portraits*, Le Chêne, Paris, 1979. 61–65 photos.

'André Kertész: In Everything I Photograph
There Is the Human Touch', pp. 115–129, in
Nude: Theory, edited by Jain Kelly, Lustrum
Press, New York, 1979. Commentary by Kertész
on his nude photographs. 1 portrait, 9 photos.

André Kertész, text by Agathe Gaillard, 16
photos. Pierre Belfond, Paris, 1980

Voyons voir: 8 photographes, interviews
conducted by Pierre Borhan, 6 photos.
Créatis, Paris, 1980

From My Window, introduction by Peter
MacGill, New York Graphic Society, Boston,
1981; *À Ma Fenêtre*, Editions Georges Herscher,
Paris, 1982. 53 Polaroid SX 70 photos

André Kertész: A Lifetime of Perception, edited
by Jane Corkin, introduction by Ben Lifson.
150 photos. Chronology by Penelope A. Dixon.
A Key Porter Book, Harry N. Abrams, New
York, 1982

Hungarian Memories, introduction by Hilton
Kramer. 144 photos. Commentary on Kertész's
photos. A New York Graphic Society Book,
Little, Brown and Co., Boston, 1982

André Kertész, text by Attilio Colombo, Fabbri,
I Grando Fotografi, Milan, 1983

André Kertész: The Manchester Collection.
Texts by Henri Cartier-Bresson, Harold Riley,
Mark Haworth-Booth, Lady Marina Vaisey,
Weston J. Naef, Colin Ford, Charles Harbutt.
302 photos. The Manchester Collection,
Manchester, 1984

André Kertész: Magyarországon, edited by János Bodnár, 50 photos plus portraits of Kertész. Föfotó, Budapest, 1984.

Kertész on Kertész: A Self-Portrait, introduction by Peter Adam, text by André Kertész, 94 photos. Abbeville Press, New York, 1985

André Kertész, 'Photo Poche' collection, text by Danièle Sallenave, Centre National de la Photographie, Paris, 1985. Reprinted 1988 and 1996

André Kertész: Shashinshu, edited by Susan Harder and Hiroji Kubota, text by Hal Hinson, Iwanami Shoten, Tokyo, 1986. US edition: *André Kertész: Diary of Light 1912–1985*, Aperture, New York, 1987; French edition: *André Kertész: soixante-dix années de photographies*, Hologramme, Paris, 1987. 152 photos

André Kertész: Ma France, text by Pierre Bonhomme, Sandra Phillips, Jean-Claude Lemagny, Michel Frizot, Ministère de la Culture/La Manufacture, Paris, 1990; German edition: *André Kertész in Paris: Fotografien 1925–1936*, Schirmer/ Mosel, Munich, 1992. 243 photos, chronology, bibliography

André Kertész: Les Instants d'une vie. Bookking International, Paris, 1993

André Kertész: 1894–1985, text by Carole Kismaric, essay by Lloyd Fonvielle, Aperture, New York, 1993

André Kertész: 1894–1985–1994, text by Kincses Károly, Miklos Matyassy, Pierre Borhan, interview with André Kertész by Bela Raffay and Lajos Magasitz, Magyar Fotografiai Muzeum/Pelikan Kiado, Budapest, 1994. 123 photos, chronology, bibliography of Hungarian texts

André Kertész: la biographie d'une oeuvre, text by Pierre Borhan, Laszlo Beke, Dominique Baqué and Jane Livingstone, Éditions du Seuil, Paris, 1994. 355 photos, chronology, bibliography, exhibitions, index. US edition: *André Kertész: His Life and Work*, Bulfinch, Boston, 1994; Japanese edition: *André Kertész*, Metropolitan Museum of Photography, Tokyo, 1995

André Kertész: le photographe à l'oeuvre, text by Evelyne Rogniat, Presses Universitaires de Lyon, Lyons; Presses de la Sorbonne Nouvelle, Paris, 1997

Deux études sur les distorsions de André Kertész, text by Frédéric Lambert and Jean-Pierre Esquenazi, L'Harmattan, Paris, 1998

André Kertész, text by Noël Bourcier, Phaidon, London, 2001

André Kertész: Made in USA, text by Alain d'Hooghe, PC Editions, Paris, 2003

La Savoie d'André Kertész, text by Jean and Renée Nicolas, Pascal Lemaître. La Fontaine de Siloé, Montmélian, 2004

André Kertész: The Early Years, text by Robert Gurbo and Bruce Silverstein, W.W. Norton, New York, 2005

Revue Télérama: André Kertész, Eugène Atget, Walker Evans (boxed set), Télérama, Paris, 2010

André Kertész: Paris, automne 1963, Flammarion, Paris, 2013

Exhibition catalogues

Kertész at Long Island University, text by Nathan Resnick, Long Island University, New York, 1962

André Kertész, Photographies, introduction by Alix Gambier, Bibliothèque Nationale, Paris, 1963

André Kertész, Photographer, text by John Szarkowski, 64 photos. Museum of Modern Art, New York, 1964

André Kertész: Fotografien, 1913–1971, by Rune Hassner, Moderna Museet, Stockholm, 1971

André Kertész: Photographs, introduction by Andrew Szegedy-Maszak, Davison Art Center, Wesleyan University, Middletown, CT, 1976. 65 photos

André Kertész, introduction by Pierre de Fenoÿl, 78 photos. Centre National d'Art et de Culture Georges Pompidou/ Contrejour, Paris, 1977

Kertész & Harbutt: Sympathetic Explorations, essay by Andy Grundberg, 24 photos by Kertész, 24 photos by Charles Harbutt. Plains Art Museum, Moorhead, Minnesota, 1978

André Kertész: An Exhibition of Photographs from the Centre Georges Pompidou, Paris, introduction by Colin Ford, 39 photos. Arts Council of Great Britain, London, 1979

André Kertész, Master of Photography, by Brooks Johnson, 44 black and white photos, 5 colour photos, chronology. The Chrysler Museum, Norfolk, Virginia, 1982

André Kertész: Form and Feeling, by Keith F. Davis, 16 photos. Hallmark Gallery, Kansas City, 1983

André Kertész: A Ninetieth Birthday Celebration, National Museum of Photography, Film and Television, Bradford, 1984

André Kertész: Of Paris and New York, text by Sandra Phillips, David Travis and Weston J. Naef, Art Institute of Chicago, Metropolitan Museum of Art, New York, and Thames & Hudson, London, 1985. 305 illustrations; 192 photos

André Kertész: Vintage Photographs, Edwynn Houk Gallery, Chicago, 1985

Kertész on Kertész: A Self-Portrait, introduction by Peter Adam, comments by Kertész, Abbeville Press, New York, 1985. 94 photos, chronology

André Kertész: Photographe, text by René Huyghe and Jean-Paul Scarpitta, Institut de France, Musée Jacquemart-André, Paris, 1987

Stranger to Paris, by Robert Enright, Jane Corkin Gallery, Toronto, 1992. Modern catalogue of the exhibition at the gallery Au Sacre du Printemps (1927), 40 photos

Paris, text by Claudio Marra and Bettina Rheims, Photology, Milan, 1993. 24 photos

André Kertész in Focus, text by Weston Naef, Robert Gurbo, Charles Hogan, Sylvia Plachy and David Travis, 55 photos from the collection of the J. Paul Getty Museum, Malibu, CA, 1994

L'intime plaisir de lire, text by Turzio Silvana, Trans Photographic Press, Lagny-sur-Marne, 1998

André Kertész & Avant-Garde Photography of the Twenties & Thirties, Annely Juda Fine Art, London, 1999

André Kertész: The Mirror as Muse, Stephen Daiter Gallery, Chicago, 1999

André Kertész: New York State of Mind, Stephen Daiter Gallery, Chicago, 2001

André Kertész: Observations, Thoughts, Reflections, Stephen Daiter Gallery, Chicago, 2005

André Kertész, text by Sarah Greenough, Robert Gurbo, Sarah Kennel, National Gallery of Art, Washington DC; Princeton University Press, Princeton, NJ, 2005

L'odyssée d'une icône: trois photographies d'André Kertész, text by Anne de Mondenard, Actes Sud, Arles; Maison Européenne de la Photographie, Paris, 2006

André Kertész: The Polaroids, text by Robert Gurbo and Eelco Wolf, W. W. Norton, New York and London, 2007

André Kertész, text by Michel Frizot and Annie-Laure Wanaverbecq, Éditions du Jeu de Paume/Hazan, Paris, 2010

Lire, écrire, photographier: Émile Zola/André Kertész, text by François Bon, Éditions du Jeu de Paume, Paris, 2010

Periodicals

André Kertész's photographs were reproduced in magazines and newspapers in Hungary from 1917 onwards; he continued this work in France and then in the USA. Here is a list of magazines and journals that published his photographs:

1917: first photograph published in *Érdekes Ujság*, in Hungary

1925: first cover for *Érdekes Ujság*

Parisian period (1928–1936):

Vu, Bifur, l'Illustration, Art et Médecine, L'Art Vivant, L'Intransigeant, Le Matin, Uhu, Variétés, The Times, The Sphere, The Sketch, La Nazionale, Berliner Illustrirte Zeitung, Die Dame, Frankfurter Illustrierte, Das Illustrierte Blatt, Kölnischer Illustrierte Zeitung, Münchner Illustrierte Presse, Neue Jugend, Photographie, Das Tageblatt

American period (1936 to 1962, when he stopped doing commercial work):

The American Magazine, Collier's, Coronet, Harper's Bazaar, Life, Look, Town and Country, Vogue.

From 1949 to 1962, he had an exclusive contract with Condé Nast Publications and worked primarily for *House and Garden* in that period.

Selected Exhibitions

Solo exhibitions

1927 Au Sacre du Printemps, Paris.

1937 PM Gallery, New York.

1946 Art Institute of Chicago.

1962 Long Island University, New York.

1963 Modern Age Studio, New York. Bibliothèque Nationale, Paris.

1964 Museum of Modern Art, New York.

1971 Moderna Museet, Stockholm. Magyar Nemzeti Galéria, Budapest.

1972 The Photographers' Gallery, London. Valokuvamuseo, Helsinki.

1973 Hallmark Gallery, New York. Light Gallery, New York.

1975 Rencontres Internationales de la Photographie, Arles.

1976 Wesleyan University, Middletown, CT. French Cultural Services, New York.

1977 Centre National d'Art et de Culture Georges Pompidou, Paris.

1978 *Kertész & Harbutt: Sympathetic Explorations*, Plains Art Museum, Moorhead, Minnesota. Light Gallery, New York. Simon Lowinsky Gallery, San Francisco.

1979 Serpentine Gallery, London. Kiva Gallery of Photography, Boston. Galerie Municipale du Château d'Eau, Toulouse.

1980 Salford University, Salford, UK. Jerusalem Art Museum. Galerie Agathe Gaillard, Paris.

1981 Jane Corkin Gallery, Toronto. Rencontres Internationales de la Photographie, Arles.

1982 Canadian Centre for Photography, Toronto. Chrysler Museum, Norfolk, Virginia. Susan Harder Gallery, New York.

1983 *André Kertész: Distortions*, Pace/MacGill Gallery, New York. *André Kertész: Color*, Susan Harder Gallery, New York. *André Kertész: Form and Feeling*, Nelson-Atkins Museum of Art, Kansas City, MO. Berner Photo-Galerie, Berne.

1984 *André Kertész: Photographs from the Manchester Collection*, Witkin Gallery, New York.

1985 *André Kertész: Of Paris and New York*, Art Institute of Chicago; Metropolitan Museum, New York; Palais de Tokyo, Paris (1986).

1986 *Distorsions*, Fondation Nationale de la Photographie, Lyons.

1987 *Diary of Light*, International Center of Photography, New York.

1987–88 *André Kertész, photographe*, Musée Jacquemart-André, Paris.

1990 *André Kertész, Ma France*, Palais de Tokyo, Paris. Touring exhibition (Lyons, Nice, Charleroi, Barcelona, Ljubljana, Braga, Vandoeuvre-lès-Nancy, Prague, Chalon-sur-Saône, Brest, Huesca, Bath, Chambéry, Milan, Istanbul), organized by the Mission du Patrimoine Photographique.

1998 *André Kertész: L'intime plaisir de lire*, Galerie Fnac Forum, Paris. Touring exhibition through France and Europe.

2004 *André Kertész et la Hongrie*, Mois de la Photo exhibition, Hungarian Institute, Paris.

2005 *André Kertész*, National Gallery of Art, Washington, DC, and Los Angeles County Museum of Art. *André Kertész: La Savoie entre ciel et terre*, Espace Malraux, Scène Nationale de Chambéry et de la Savoie, France.

2006 *L'odyssée d'une icône: trois photographies d'André Kertész*, Maison Européenne de la Photographie, Paris.

2007 *André Kertész: The Polaroids*, Bruce Silverstein Gallery, New York.

2007–8 Southwest Museum of Photography, Daytona Beach, FL. *André Kertész: Seven Decades*, J. Paul Getty Museum, Malibu, CA.

2008 *André Kertész*, Portland Museum of Art, OR.

2009 *André Kertész*, Reykjavik Museum of Photography, Iceland. *On Reading: André Kertész*, The Photographers' Gallery, London.

2010–11 *André Kertész*, Jeu de Paume, Paris.

2015 *A Retrospective by André Kertész*, Art Basel 46, Bruce Silverstein Gallery, Basel, Switzerland.

2017 *André Kertész*, Sungkok Art Museum, Seoul.

Group exhibitions

1928 Premier Salon Indépendant de la Photographie, Théâtre des Champs-Elysées, Paris.

1929 *Film und Foto*, Deutscher Werkbund, Stuttgart.

1932 *Modern European Photography*, Julien Levy Gallery, New York.

1934 *Groupe annuel des photographes*, Galerie de la Pléiade, Paris. *Photographies*, Salon Leleu, Paris.

1937 *Photography 1839–1937*, Museum of Modern Art, New York.

1941 *Image of Freedom*, Museum of Modern Art, New York.

1967 *The Concerned Photographer*, Riverside Museum, New York.

1968 *The Concerned Photographer*, Maisura, Tokyo.

1970 Expo 1970, US Pavilion, Tokyo.

1976 *Photographs from the Julien Levy Collection*, Art Institute of Chicago, Chicago.

1977 *Documenta VI,* Kassel, Germany.

1986 *La Nouvelle Photographie en France*, Poitiers, Arles, and Carcassonne, France.

1989 *L'Invention d'un Art*, Musée National d'Art Moderne, Centre Georges Pompidou, Paris.

1989–90 *Histoire de voir*, Centre National de la Photographie, Palais de Tokyo, Paris.

1992 *J'aime la France*, Printemps Ginza, Tokyo. Touring exhibition (1993–94) to Osaka, Nagoya, Hiroshima, Yamagata (Japan), Seoul (South Korea), Barcelona (Spain), Sydney, Perth and Brisbane (Australia).

1994 *Spectacle: De la scène à l'écran*, Hôtel de Sully, Paris.

2004 *Linked Journeys: Hungarian Photographs from Around the World* (collection of the Hungarian Museum of Photography, Budapest). Collegium Hungaricum, Vienna.

2005 *Neues Sehen in Berlin: Fotografie der Zwanziger Jahre*, Kunstbibliothek, Berlin.

2010–11 *Émile Zola photographe / André Kertész: L'intime plaisir de lire*, Château de Tours, France.

2015 *I Hear Your Voice Reflected in a Glass and It Sounds Like It Is Inside of Me*, Carlier Gebauer, Berlin.